SIR GEORGE OTTO TREVELYAN

George Otto Trevelyan

Portrait by Frank Holl, now at Trinity College, Cambridge.

SIR GEORGE OTTO TREVELYAN

A MEMOIR

BY HIS SON

GEORGE MACAULAY TREVELYAN

WITH ILLUSTRATIONS

LONGMANS, GREEN AND CO.

LONDON · NEW YORK · TORONTO

1932

LONGMANS, GREEN AND CO. LTD.

39 PATERNOSTER ROW, LONDON, E.C.4
6 OLD COURT HOUSE STREET, CALCUTTA
53 NICOL ROAD, BOMBAY
36A MOUNT ROAD, MADRAS

LONGMANS, GREEN AND CO.

55 FIFTH AVENUE, NEW YORK
221 EAST 20TH STREET, CHICAGO
88 TREMONT STREET, BOSTON
128–132 UNIVERSITY AVENUE, TORONTO

Made in Great Britain

PREFACE

THE posthumous penalty for very long life is that those who knew a man when he was active in the world have long passed away when his biography or memoir comes to be written. When at last it appears, it belongs not to the realm of quasi-contemporary happenings but to the realm of history. Yet for some, history, too, has its charms. My father lived until 1928, but his first literary successes as a Cambridge undergraduate had been won before the American Civil War broke out, and moreover he had given up politics and retired into the country thirty years before he died. He belongs, therefore, to the generation of the late or even of the middle Victorians. If he had written his own memoirs, he would have made the London society of the 'sixties and 'seventies as actual to the reader as he made the equally brilliant society in which Charles Fox passed his youth.

Unhappily he neglected to do so, and it is useless for another to attempt to write his 'Life and Times.' Many years ago he told me that he did not wish his Life to be written. Later he said that I could do as I thought fit in the matter. In any case he disliked long biographies, and I have followed what

I am sure was his desire in confining the record to a brief and personal memoir.

He belonged to a type that flourished most in the reign of Queen Victoria, the literary man who was also a politician, the politician and literary man who was also an historian. As a bygone type he may interest those of a different day ; as an individual he may interest them even more, for in him we see the classical and literary culture of that age, and the very strong influence of his uncle, working upon a strongly marked personal temperament that was quite his own.

My thanks are due to my cousins, Mrs. Abel Smith and Mr. Frank Dugdale, for the free use of his intimate letters to his sisters. I have also to thank Lady Desborough, Lord Crewe, Mrs. Henry Sidgwick and Mrs. Yates Thompson for the use of letters, and Mr. Arthur Scribner, Mr. Edward Graham and the Butler family, the *Times* and the *Saturday Review* for the use of copyright material.

CAMBRIDGE,
November, 1931.

CONTENTS

LIST OF ILLUSTRATIONS

CHAPTER I

ORIGINS. FAMILY LIFE. SCHOOL DAYS

THE Trevelyans are a very old family. All families, we must suppose, are equally old, whether we adopt the Darwinian or the Fundamentalist view of human origins ; but ' an old family,' I take it, can trace an ascent far back in the catalogue of gentry. That much the Trevelyans can do, as three volumes of their *Papers*, published by the Camden Society, bear witness.

From time immemorial a water-mill has stood over a Cornish stream, where its sweet water falls into the estuary of the sea, in the parish of St. Veep, a few miles above Fowey town. The ancient Britons called the spot Trevelyan, which I am told means ' the place of the mill.' A farm near it was already called by that name in Doomsday Book. It is recorded that in the reign of Henry III, and it is probable that even earlier, Trevelyan was in the hands of people who had taken their name from it. Thence they spread over Cornwall and the neighbouring counties. In the days of the rival Roses, a John Trevelyan, sometime Member of Parliament, dabbled in the muddy political waters of that period. Being staunch for

B

Lancaster, he was satirised in Yorkist lampoons
as 'the Cornish chough who oft with his train
[tail feathers] hath made our eagle blind'—the
' eagle' being apparently that least aquiline of all
our monarchs, the poor, draggled dove, Henry VI.
One year, when the white rose was blooming,
Trevelyan was arraigned for a piracy of which
he had been guilty when his party was in the
ascendant. It was such an act as any lusty
gentleman of the coastwise counties would commit
as a matter of course in that litigious but lawless
age. It seems that his ship had seized a richly
laden Catalan galley that lay at anchor off
Plymouth. Not a very heroic exploit, but, in
the language of so competent an authority as
Mr. Kingsford, John Trevelyan belonged to the
'school of English seamen' and of 'west country
piracy' which in the fullness of time produced
Francis Drake. Even so, our ancestor has not
won his way into the 'Dictionary of National
Biography,' nor has any other of his surname
who flourished prior to the nineteenth century.
Generation after generation went by, and neither
the world of politics nor the world of letters
heard talk of the Trevelyans. For five hundred
years and more they went on, from father to son,
pursuing the quiet life of country gentlemen in
the remote south-west, farming, collecting rents
and taking game, surviving in their middle station
the storms that were sweeping away the great
families, as the brushwood survives when the oak
is rooted up.

NETTLECOMBE, IN SOMERSET, ABOUT 1818.

But by the latter part of the eighteenth century they had obtained a position of wealth and local importance at the two ends of England. Sir John Trevelyan was the owner of two considerable estates : Nettlecombe in Somerset, the old family property which had belonged to his Lancastrian ancestor, and Wallington in Northumberland, which came to him in 1777 as a result of marriage relationship with the Blacketts, the principal Tyneside magnates of that era. The story recorded in this volume will end at Wallington, but it begins at Nettlecombe. From Nettlecombe came my grandfather, Sir Charles Edward Trevelyan, who left his mark on the Home and Indian Civil Service, married Macaulay's sister, and was the father of George Otto.

Nettlecombe, a Tudor country-house with the mediaeval parish church upon its lawn, and the dependent village of Monksilver decently withdrawn from its view, lay close under the Quantocks, as it still lies to-day, a haunt of ancient peace. From the hillocks of the park, the Bristol Channel is visible four miles off. A mile up the valley, in a nook of the wooded hills, lay the secluded Rectory, properly filled in Jane Austen's day by the Rev. George Trevelyan, sometime Archdeacon of Taunton, younger son of Sir John, the Baronet of Nettlecombe. My grandfather, the future Sir Charles, born in 1807, was merely the child of the Rectory, though destined to win a baronetcy by his public services, and to end life as squire of Wallington owing to failure of progeny in the

direct line. The parson's son was a favourite with
his grandfather, old Sir John, up at the 'big
house,' who allowed his grandson to 'sport over
the manor.' And so, while the sordid tragedy of
Peterloo and the sordid comedy of Queen Caroline
were convulsing Lancashire and London, in remote
Somerset, untroubled by these rumours of a darker
world, the boy was roaming the coppices, armed
with an old flint-lock that would better have
served a tall grenadier at Minden. He used
afterwards to tell how one day ' the woodcocks
were hopping round him in the spinney like
sparrows,' and this barbarous old weapon would
not give fire, till he was almost crying for vexation.
I remember him sixty years later, on his Northumbrian estate, carrying his modern breech-loader in
an old-fashioned and rather alarming manner,
grasped with both hands behind his back.
Perhaps he used to carry his piece so, when he
was dreaming on things to come, in his solitary
boyhood's rambles in the Somerset spinneys when
George was King. But he could be on the alert
when he wanted, and was no mean sportsman.
As a young man he was one of the most famous
hog-spears in India.

His schooling was in Somerset, until in 1820 he
went to Charterhouse, and thence in due time to
the East India Company's College at Haileybury,
where a dormitory has been named after him. In
1826 he entered the Company's service, at the age
of nineteen. It was characteristic of him that he
was preparing to make his way to India on horse-

back, through Persia and the mountains of Baluchistan ; but the Company forbade the rash expedition. He went out round the Cape by the usual six months' voyage, and had to be content with riding from Bombay to Calcutta. He was then sent up to Delhi as First Assistant to the English Resident there. In that capacity, at the age of twenty-one, he took the most courageous step of his whole career ; he denounced his superior, a man of great authority and popularity in the Company's service, for systematically taking bribes from Indians.

My grandfather, at that time without connections in the Anglo-Indian world, was left alone as a mere lad to face the consequences of his act, without a friend to advise or encourage him.

A perfect storm was raised against the accuser [wrote Macaulay in a private letter a few years afterwards]. He was almost everywhere abused and generally cut. But with a firmness and ability scarcely ever seen in any man so young, he brought his proof forward, and, after an enquiry of some weeks, fully made out his case.

The Resident was forced to leave the service, a broken man. The affair was an important step in setting the high standard of purity which has marked English administration in India. That standard was not established in a day. The evils against which Clive strove so manfully in the era of the ' nabobs ' had been scotched but not killed when my grandfather first went out, and the principle for which he took his stand was by no means to the taste of all Anglo-Indians in the days

of Jos Sedley. Hence the fury that he provoked and the danger in which he stood for a
while. He emerged triumphant, under the protection of the Governor-General, Lord William
Bentinck, who had ordered the inquiry, and
after its outcome became his patron and his friend.[1]

My grandfather was one of those utterly fearless
and disinterested men, who have their own
standards and always act up to them. Our
average standards in some matters may be higher
now than then, but men who can stand alone are
no commoner. They are never common, but
England a hundred years ago had more of them
perhaps than most countries and most times.
There was then a type of man in whom the best
administrative tradition of the English country
gentleman had been stiffened by the self-discipline
and enlarged by the philanthropic zeal of
Evangelicalism, a movement of which the best
products were seen among the laity. Such men
were England's most effective instrument in
carrying through the solid reforms of the early
nineteenth century. My grandfather was affected
by that twofold heritage of the country gentleman
and the evangelical, but much of his mind and
character was purely personal to himself. He
was not a type but an individual. He had the
defects of his qualities. Inconsiderate rashness
in pursuit of a scheme of public welfare sometimes
brought him into serious conflict with the authori-

---

[1] The official papers of the inquiry can be studied in *Papers transmitted
from India*, by C. E. Trevelyan, Esq., published by J. L. Cox, 1830.

SIR CHARLES TREVELYAN
About 1870.

ties, whom he usually served so well. His worst error of that sort, which gave a serious check to his career, was made in 1859, when he was old in official experience. Yet thirty years before, at an age when other lads are working for their University degree, he had conducted this Delhi business, so delicate and so dangerous, with the wariness and wisdom of a veteran Perhaps the sense that his all in this world was at stake inspired him with unwonted prudence.

Once more I recall him, in his strong old age as squire of Wallington, with his tall, wiry frame, his snow-white hair, his face as rugged as a sea-worn rock, its deep lines instinct with energy and power, the eyes alive for every happening. Though always talking or brooding over some scheme of improvement, he was kind and un-censorious in the ordinary ways of life. His evangelicalism had by that time become an attitude of the soul rather than a dogmatic creed ; at least it was tempered by reason and good sense, and by wide reading conducted on plans originally suggested to him by Macaulay.

But he was a rough diamond when my grand-mother, Hannah More Macaulay, first met him at Calcutta in 1834 and began to polish him. Their Indian courtship was described by Macaulay in a long letter to a sister at home. My father, in his ' Life of Macaulay ' forty years later, printed much of that letter, but not all of it, my grand-father being then alive. It now belongs to the remote past, and I therefore propose to print here

an excerpt containing sentences which my father
omitted, and so give a first-hand unexpurgated
account of my grandfather when he came down
from his solitary life in Upper India to the great
world of the Governor-General's court, and took
my grandmother's heart by storm.

His reading [wrote Macaulay on December 7, 1834] has
been very confined.   He has very little English literature,
and, which surprises me greatly, does not know a word of
French.   But to the little that he has read he has brought
a mind as active and restless as Lord Brougham's and
much more judicious and honest.   He has no small talk.
His mind is full of schemes of moral and political improve-
ments, and his zeal boils over in all his talk.   His topics
even in courtship are steam navigation, the education of
the natives, the equalization of the sugar duties, the sub-
stitution of the Roman for the Arabic alphabet in the
oriental languages.   His principles I believe to be excellent and his temper very sweet.   His own religious feelings
are ardent, like all his feelings, even to enthusiasm, but he
is by no means intolerant with regard to others.   He has
faults, certainly, but they are, for the most part, faults
which time, society, domestic life, and a visit which in a
few years he will pay to England, are almost certain
to correct.   He is rash and uncompromising in public
matters.   If he were a wrong-headed and narrow-minded
man he would be a perfect nuisance.   But he has so
strong an understanding that, though he often goes too
fast, he scarcely ever goes in a wrong direction.

His manners are odd, blunt almost to roughness at
times, and at other times awkward even to sheepishness.
But when you consider that during the important years
of his life from twenty to twenty-five or thereabouts
Trevelyan was in a remote province of India, where his
whole time was divided between public business and field
sports, and where he seldom saw a European gentleman

and never a European lady, you will not wonder at this. Everybody says that he has been greatly improved since he came down to Calcutta. Under Nancy's [Hannah's] tuition he is improving fast ; his voice, his face and all his gestures express a softness quite new to him. There is nothing vulgar about him. He has as yet no great tact or knowledge of the world ; but these drawbacks, were they six times more serious, would be trifling when compared with the excellencies of his character. He is a man of genius, a man of honour, a man of rigid integrity and of a very kind heart.

As to his person, nobody can call him handsome, and Nancy, I suppose in order to anticipate the verdict of others, pronounces him ugly. He has, however, a very good figure and always looks like a gentleman, particularly on horseback. He is very active and athletic, and is renowned as a great master in the most exciting and perilous of field sports, the spearing of wild boars. His face has a most characteristic expression of ardour and impetuosity, which makes his countenance very interesting to me, and, if she would own it, to Nancy too.

Birth is a thing I care nothing about. But his family is one of the oldest and best in England. Money is a more important matter, and there I think that Nancy is fortunate. He has five thousand pounds in England. The salary here is at present about £2,000 sterling a year and will, in all probability, be soon increased. If he lives there can be no doubt of his rising rapidly to the most lucrative places in the Indian Government.

From this last sentence, and from other more intimate sentences in which Macaulay poured out his heart, it is clear that at the time of his sister's engagement and marriage at Calcutta, he expected that, on his own return to England a few years later, the Trevelyans would remain in India and that he would be separated for life, with a few short intervals, from the sister upon whom he had so imprudently lavished his affections, and without whose company he did not expect to be able to live with happiness. It was this that rendered his conduct admirable in promoting their mutual attachment from the first, at a stage when a few cold words or looks on his part would have frightened off a lover always scrupulous and at that time scarcely venturing to hope.

But Macaulay reaped an unexpected reward for his unselfishness. The family circle which he helped to create, not expecting to participate in its happiness, became for the rest of his life a real 'home' to him, so far as a bachelor in lodgings can call another house his home. The Trevelyans returned with him to England in 1838 on furlough, and stayed on there, contrary to expectation, because my grandfather was in January, 1840, appointed Assistant Secretary to the Treasury, although it was most unusual to make exchanges between the Home and the Company's services. He remained in that leading position in Whitehall for twenty years, and only returned to India when the last sands of his brother-in-law's life were just running out.[1]

The pages of Macaulay's journal show that, except during his holidays out of town, the bachelor of the Albany went to the Trevelyans' house, or

---

[1] In October 1921 my father wrote to Lord Rosebery: ' When my father was a young man in high office, keeping common house with Macaulay, he used to bring Macaulay printed matter—reports and minutes—and at first he was rather puzzled and piqued by his brother-in-law casting his eyes down the pages more than rapidly ; but he soon found that he had mastered, and for a time remembered, the actual words and sentences.'

received them in his lodgings, most days of the week. His relations to his sister were unchanged by her marriage, and my grandfather became like a younger brother to him, but with much more reverence and appreciation than most younger brothers feel called upon to display. And Macaulay's relations to his nieces Margaret and Alice and to his nephew George became at least a very good substitute for the relationship of father to children. A happier, a more affectionate, a more book-loving, talk-loving, laughter-loving household there was not in Britain, especially whenever ' Uncle Tom ' came round to make up the number. If in some societies Macaulay was sometimes ' overpowering,' there was never any such feeling in the household at Clapham—nor indeed are Trevelyans at any age very easily ' overpowered.'

My father was born on July 20, 1838, at Rothley Temple, in Leicestershire, where Macaulay had been born thirty-eight years before; it was the home of the Babingtons, kinsmen and friends of the Macaulays. My father was baptised George, after his paternal grandfather. Otto was also an old family name among the Trevelyans : there was an Odo Trevelyan as early as 1362, and my father had an Uncle Otto. His elder sister, Margaret, the 'Baba' of Macaulay's journals, had been born in India at the end of 1835 ; she became the second wife of Henry Holland, first Lord Knutsford. My father's younger sister, Alice, was more of his age and was his principal playmate in childhood ; she afterwards became Mrs. Stratford Dugdale. Counting ' Uncle Tom,' Sir Charles Trevelyan's family numbered six, and every one of them was deeply interested in books, not excepting by this time Sir Charles himself. When the talk was not running on politics, it ran on history and literature, and always in a stream of eagerness and merriment. The jokes, the puns, the laughter turned on familiar figures in fiction or history or in the public life of the day. Thanks to Uncle Tom, the past of England, of Rome, of Greece was to them all, parents and children alike, as many-coloured and actual as the present. It was this daily, loving familiarity with an unseen world that produced ' The Lays of Ancient Rome '—and everything that is of most value in my father's own writings in verse or prose.

The instigation to solid reading in order to keep pace with Uncle Tom's jokes and allusions was enough to give Margaret, Alice and George ' strong bookmindedness ' without making them pedants or prigs. My father's sisters were quite up to the game. The ladies of that day, not being in bondage to schools, colleges and examinations, often had a better notion of literature and history than that given to some of their granddaughters by classes and text books ; and in the absence of games and motoring and other modern pastimes, many of them read great masses of history and poetry for pleasure. That was true of my father's mother and of his two sisters, as well as of my mother when she came on to the

scene. The families that then lived round
Clapham Common, especially the Thorntons of
Battersea Rise, the next-door neighbours and
intimate friends of the Trevelyans, formed a highly
cultivated as well as philanthropic and ' evangelical ' society.

Naturally enough, to my father's boyish mind,
the Victorian present appeared chiefly as a con-
tinuation of the past, a glory of renascent Whigdom
and judicious reform, carrying on the well-known tale
of English history unbroken into another delightful
age. But neither was he tempted to regard life,
literature or politics as being all beer and skittles.
His uncle was a notorious worker, and as to his
father, every weekday Sir Charles disappeared
after an early breakfast, riding in from Clapham
to Whitehall to transact the nation's money affairs,
with a sharp look-out against aristocratic jobbers
and middle-class contractors, creating the standards
of the British Treasury in the nineteenth century.
Sir Charles had the right to two months' holiday
in the year, but never took more than one. And
in the summer of the Mutiny, after sending his
family into the country, he spent his own holiday
in London, waiting there for the earliest daily
news from India out of sheer anxiety for the event.

And so the talk heard and overheard by my
father from his earliest years was inspired by
interest in public affairs, zeal for administrative
reform and scrupulousness about public money.
The political atmosphere that surrounded him
from childhood was not radicalism, speculative or

class-conscious, but the ideas of the reforming public servant. In that Macaulay and his brother-in-law saw eye to eye. Together they pushed on the movement for substituting competitive examination for jobbery in appointments to the Civil Service, first in India, then in England.[1]

To Sir Charles Trevelyan's children and to Zachary Macaulay's son, Evangelicalism was the family religion, as such respected and as such resented and criticized. At least there were no other religions in the field. My grandfather read the Bible and family prayers in his deep sonorous voice and loved reading them, and the rest loved to hear him. Macaulay was well up in the Fathers, in Pascal and in the Anglican Divines, besides having the Bible 'at his fingers' ends.' He relished the religious controversies of history, because they were controversies and because they were part of history. His pencil scored notes thick along the margins of such books as the Works

---

[1] Sir Charles, though a reformer by temperament, was far too good a civil servant to be a party man. Among his papers is a letter written to him by Disraeli after the defeat of his famous budget of 1852, which says: 'My dear Sir Charles, I cannot leave the Treasury without expressing to you my sense of the zealous, efficient and friendly manner in which you have aided and supported me in my attempt to discharge the duties of Chancellor of the Exchequer. Your suggestive sympathy with the views of financial and administrative reform, which I endeavoured to carry into effect, often encouraged me amid the great difficulties with which I had to contend, and notwithstanding the present check I have such confidence in their soundness that I doubt not their general purpose will ultimately by some hand or other be accomplished. Though you may afford to my successors the same invaluable assistance which you accorded to me, I assure you none of them will more appreciate such services, or more cherish their remembrance than yours sincerely, B. Disraeli.' Palmerston opposed, but Gladstone forwarded and eventually completed the realisation of Sir Charles's schemes for the reform of the Civil Service by Competitive Examination. He received his K.C.B. in 1848, and his Baronetcy in 1874.

of Conyers Middleton, Warburton's 'Julian' and Joseph Milner's 'History of the Church.' He detested Milner as 'dishonest and malevolent,' and he did not explore Middleton and his orthodox opponents solely with a view to eliciting the truth about miracles ; but he loved to sit in his arm-chair as judge of the combat, to enforce marginally fair play on both sides and to appreciate as a brother swordsman the shrewd laying on of 'apostolic blows and knocks.' Macaulay never put on record his ultimate convictions on religion, and very probably never formulated them to himself. Perhaps the term 'agnostic,' in the stricter sense of that misused word, might have fitted him. He did not carry his celebrated 'cocksureness' into the sphere of religion, and perhaps for that reason neither wrote nor talked about it. It is only the marginal notes in his books which show how well-read he was in theology. In the last sentence of one of Middleton's controversial pieces occur these words :

But if *to live strictly and think freely ; to practise what is moral and to believe what is rational*, be consistent with the sincere profession of Christianity, then I shall acquit myself like one of its truest professors.

Macaulay has underlined the words I have put in italics and has written in the margin : ' Haec est absoluta et perfecta philosophi vita.'

My father, from boyhood to old age, treated religion respectfully but shyly. Since he did not understand Christianity, he left it alone with little remark. He recognised it as a great fact in the history of England, and in human nature—at least in the nature of others. In a purely negative sense he was a hearty Protestant, though he abhorred intolerance in that or any other cause. But his religious reading lay in the less mystical parts of the doctrines attributed to Socrates, in Epictetus and in Carlyle's ' Sartor ' ; all these he read and re-read, in part at least ' for edification.' He had the Victorian belief in the emphatic difference between right and wrong conduct, wherein he did not take much account of nuances. Without being censorious, he had the definite moral standards of his family and later of all his ' set '—the Sidgwicks, Edward Bowen and the rest. The battle for religious equality which was fought and won in his early manhood interested him a great deal more than religion, and a great deal more than those religious controversies in which his uncle had sought extra food to satisfy his voracious appetite for reading.

In his later years, as squire of Wallington, my father used occasionally to attend matins at Cambo Church, of which his father had erected the tower. He usually read the Old Testament Lesson ; he knew how to make the most of the grand old words, and I recall the obvious pleasure with which on these occasions he stressed the diphthong in the word ' Isaiah.'

If reverence is the essence of religion, my father had it in plenty for the nobler men and actions of history, which he idealised to a degree that was at once his strength and weakness as an historian.

To him 'Men's History and Man's History was a
perpetual Evangel.' In that respect at least, his
attitude to history and to life was less distant from
Carlyle's than from Gibbon's, both of whom and
everything about whom he read with unwearied
love from the time he left Cambridge till he could
read no more.

I have perhaps been going too fast in describing
my father's attitude in these matters, before I
have narrated his boyhood and youth. But in
essentials the bent of his mind was fixed from the
earliest years. His uncle and the household at
Clapham had sowed the seed before ever he went
to school. Harrow and Trinity speeded and
spread its growth, but I doubt if anything could
have stopped or diverted it.

He went first as a boarder to a private school of
no particular merit at Little Berkhamsted in
Hertfordshire. Such account as he used to give
me of it bore out the pictures drawn in 'Vanity
Fair' and 'Harry Richmond' of that old type of
school, since disappeared. There were thirty boys
and there was no one to teach them but the Head
Master, who was also the parson of the parish, his
wife, and the usher. The usher was employed on
almost menial terms, a man not at all on a social
equality with the 'under-master' of a private school
of our own day. The equivocal position of the
'usher,' easily detected by the hard eye of boyhood,
led the unfortunate man to pose as a 'gentleman'
with would-be modish chatter, such as Thackeray

c

would have swooped upon to appropriate for his
' Book of Snobs.' The school, I think, left no
impress on my father's mental powers for good or
evil. But he used always to say that he would have
grown up into a man of greater physical strength if
he had not been underfed there. The food was good
of its kind but always deficient in quantity and the
boys rose hungry from their meals. The school
game was rounders.[1]

A happier and more important stage was
reached when he went in 1851 to Harrow, then
at the height of the scholarly and intellectual
eminence which it reached under Vaughan, in
the days of

> Blayds and Merivale, Hope, Monro,
> Ridley and Hawkins years ago,
> And one that I rather think I know—

to wit Montagu Butler, who went up to Trinity a
term after my father entered Harrow. Vaughan's
pupils regarded their Head Master as a great man,
who had somehow done wonders for each and all
of them. Such was emphatically my father's
opinion, which he often expressed ; he would add
that Vaughan was no great scholar and not even
well read in general literature, but that he always
thoroughly knew the books he undertook to teach,
and had a wonderful way of fostering the literary

---

[1] In his last term there, at the age of thirteen, he writes to his father:
' Rennie has got me to write some cruel latin verses to a *real* girl who rejects
his addresses. I did them as my regular work under the form of a lover's
ode. I am to take them in to some anonymous post. She will never make
out who wrote them. She will take them to be from some real lover. For,
though only thirteen, and really pretty, she aims at being admired. This
must not be told. She will think it fun.'

G. O. Trevelyan and his Sister Alice.

instincts of others. Certainly he remade Harrow, and certainly scholarship and the love of letters flourished there under him, even after he had made Byron's old school fashionable once more. There was a great deal of the bear-garden about it, not least in the Grove under Steele, where my father was placed. But rowdyism and happy-go-lucky are no worse for the free play of letters and intellect than well-regulated routine.

Even as a small boy my father was not unhappy at Harrow, as is shown by his racy and intimate letters to his adored playmate and younger sister, Alice. He was fairly tough, stood the prescribed amount of bullying in small-boyhood, always had plenty of friends to whom he unbosomed himself freely, and lived besides a private life of book-reading with its roots at home and in the Albany. Here is a letter written in his first term, in the summer of the Great Exhibition of 1851—such as any small boy might have written to his sister, then, or a hundred years before, or after.

My dear Alice,
    I am very sorry that I did not write before but I had not time. I have been told about such funny German figures in the Exhibition. Bishop, who was once head-master, has got us a half-holiday, and, what is still better, verses let off. I walked with Ellis for nearly two hours, and spent this whole afternoon in larking with Parker who is universally liked. I shall save up my tin to buy a ten bob racket from Sam's. There is such a jolly bath here : 3 feet deep at one end and 6 at the other and 20 yards long. I have several friends and am most excessively jolly. There is a little boy here, called Mayo,

very handsome, smart and clever. He is a friend of mine. There was a boy flogged by the head of the school for spreading a report that Dr. Vaughan had cheated him. This led to a great many punishments, for all Simmy's boys have stayed outside to *hear* the operation, and got 500 lines apiece. Happily not me. I have drawn 4 beautiful pictures of a battle for you which you shall have when I see you next. Mr. Simpkinson is very facetious during school time, and sets the whole form in a roar, not at the joke but for the sake of a moment's relaxation from work, at which he gets angry, particularly since one boy laughs in an affected manner for some time afterwards.

He stayed on at Harrow till he was nineteen, immensely enjoying his last three years as one of the ' swells.' He made, indeed, a very remarkable position for himself in the rough-and-tumble old Harrow world, purely on his intellectual and social qualities, for he had no skill in athletics. He became Head of the School and Gregory Prizeman (1856),[1] swept up the school prizes as the hero of two Speech Days, and won the English Prize Poem three years running.

George [wrote Macaulay in 1857 to his friend Ellis] is buried under laurels—first in the examination, Gregory

[1] His friend, Edward Bowen, afterwards wrote the Harrow Song, ' She was a Shepherdess, O so fair,' that tells how

> The Gregory Prizeman won the maid,
> Many a year ago.
> ' For none,' she said,
> ' Will I ever wed
> But the boy who gets the Gregory Prize,
> Crosses his t's and dots his i's,
> Down in the plain below.'

This was often sung by my elder brothers with other Harrow Songs in our home, and as a child I firmly believed that was the principle on which my mother had selected her husband. I thought she must have been a very nice, quiet shepherdess, also that it was a hazardous way of choosing a partner for life, though it had turned out well in this case.

Medal, Peel Medal, every prize that he has contended
for without exception. And really he is a good modest
boy, not at all boastful or self confident. His home
indeed is not one in which a young fellow would be
likely to become a coxcomb.

And in his private journal for 1856 he notes
after Harrow Speech Day :

George was the hero of the day. All his exercises had
merit. I was much pleased with the Latin verse. The
English heroics too were good, and very well recited. I
hope and believe that he will turn out a distinguished
man. He is most amiable, and I never saw such perfect
harmony in a family as there is between him and his
sisters. In truth, none of the three ever, so far as I am
able to discover, says or does anything inconsistent with
perfect love and kindness to the others.

On the first occasion when he won the Prize
Poem, in 1855, with some spirited lines on the
' Invasions of England,' he altered the ending
after the poem had been printed, to introduce a
passage about the actual war in the Crimea, more
suitable than the original version for declamation
at Speech Day. The family conclave sat on the
proposed alterations—there was no harm in that
as the prize was already awarded. One of the
new couplets ran thus :

England, for thee we left our homes, for thee we crossed
the main,
For thee the thousand graves were dug on Varna's fatal
plain.

My grandfather proposed, in the interests of
statistical truth, to substitute the words ' two

thousand' for 'the thousand,' which he declared
to be an understatement of the victims of disease
who perished in the camp at Varna. But the
Treasury's stand for accurate enumeration was
outvoted by the literary interest represented by
the Macaulay blood.[1]

He also distinguished himself by an output of
topical English verse in imitation of Juvenal,
including some good-natured satires on certain of
his schoolfellows. In the absence of a school
paper, his verses appeared some of them in the
Harrow Gazette, and some printed on separate fly-
sheets, distributed I know not how. Already in
the forum of his own mind he was pitting himself
against Canning's 'Microcosm' and the *Etonian* of
1824 ; but it was not till he reached Cambridge
that his gift for light verse came to full flower.

In 1913 he wrote to my brother Robert :

George Russell and the Harrow masters got hold of a
manuscript copy of my Juvenal parodies of the year
1856—when I was seventeen, fifty-seven years ago—and
are printing them in the *Harrovian*. It is curious that
I had the knack of thinking in rhyme then, which I
entirely lost ten years afterwards. It is so long ago that,
to boys now at school, it would be as verses written in
1800 would have been to me !

[1] My father told me this story. I have a copy of *Prolusiones* for Speech Day,
1855, in which my grandmother has written out the new lines in place of
the last dozen printed lines. There is a tick against the disputed word ' the '
in ' the thousand.'

A Harrow story of this period is recorded in a letter my father wrote to
Lord Rosebery in 1920 : ' When Palmerston came to Harrow—riding in
white trousers, there and back—to open something or other, he said that
Harrow might be proud of having turned out Sir Robert Peel and Lord
Aberdeen. *Punch* remarked that Lord Palmerston was very modest. He
had done a great deal more than Harrow to turn out Peel and Aberdeen.'

HARRY YATES THOMPSON and SIR GEORGE TREVELYAN
at Welcombe, about 1923.

' The Harrow School Register,' profusely annotated by his own hand in extreme old age, shows how many of his schoolfellows were men whom he came across in after life, at Cambridge, in India, in politics, in society, or in country life. Against the name of Francis Storr, afterwards Sixth Form Master at Marlborough, he has written ' my great ally '—meaning, I think, at Harrow ; against Henry Strutt ' my best man ' at his wedding, and so through many other names. He particularly notes how long-lived were his Harrow friends—a healthy, prosperous lot no doubt. I remember not a few of them long afterwards as frequent visitors at Wallington—Kenelm Edward Digby, solid as a rock ; Sir William Church, the wise and benevolent old squire-doctor, President of the College of Physicians ; and last but not least Yates Thompson—' Harry Thompson '—a connoisseur of the curiosities of art and of life, who lived to be the generous, bluff, broad-bearded, outspoken friend, benefactor, and amused critic of so many generations of younger people. He and his wife were intimate friends of my father and mother to the very end. Five years before the end, in 1923, my father thus answered one of Harry's letters :

I liked your allusion to Dolly's care of you. Seventy years ago when, as two little fellows, we deliberately struck up a friendship in the Harrow cricket-ground, we little foresaw that we should be the most fortunate of men, in regard to the greatest blessing that providence had in its power to bestow.

In the August of 1857, after his last term at
Harrow had ended, he was privileged to go a
walking tour in Tirol, in the region of Heiligen
Blut, with no less a person than Montagu Butler,
five years his senior, and regarded by the world
of Harrow and by the world of Cambridge as
the paragon of the rising generation. Sixty
years on, my father wrote the following
account of it, which I am kindly permitted
to quote from his Introductory Chapter to
Mr. Graham's ' Harrow Life of Henry Montagu
Butler ' :

It was a romantic land, that Tyrol, inhabited by a
manly and handsome race ; and the national costume,
graceful and imposing in itself, recalled old engravings
of Hofer, and his compatriots, in their war of Liberation
against the Bavarian invader. Our weather was often
glorious ; and the scenery, near and remote, was different
from that of Switzerland, but hardly less enchanting,
with its distant snowcaps peering over the endless waves
of pine-forest, and its peaks of Dolomite, tawny at mid-
day, and vivid scarlet in the sunset glow. The hill-
streams swarmed with blue trout, and babbled and sang
in the keen morning air. It was the time of our lives ;
' that happy hopeful past ' (to quote the words of James
Lowell) ' when one was capable of everything, because
one had not tried anything.' We strolled, or trudged, or
clambered, sometimes with our eyes intent on the objects
around and above us, but more often discoursing with
absorbing interest, and unquenchable animation, on
matters which we knew about, or at all events which we
cared about. Across this immense stretch of years I
can still recall a discussion on the question whether
Doctor Arnold, or Doctor Vaughan, was the greater
Headmaster ; and a protracted, and at last heated,

debate over certain episodes in the private and public
conduct of King David as recorded in the Books of
Samuel and of Chronicles. On one afternoon my
companion beguiled the last mile or two of a day's walk
by a spirited epitome of the story of Uncas in ' The Last
of the Mohicans.' He fascinated me by his ardour and
eloquence ; but I remember thinking that the manu-
facture of a high-minded, humane, and chivalrous hero
out of a Red Indian of North America was a feat beyond
even Montagu Butler's power of idealising. From time
to time he faithfully redeemed his promise to in-
doctrinate me in Cambridge modes of life, and study,
and duty ; and I carried to the University a store of
good resolutions, deserving a better fate than for the
most part too surely awaited them, which had been
instilled into my mind by the wisest, and most attractive,
of Mentors.

Half way through our time we had a touch of hard-
ship, with a cheerful and satisfactory issue. After one
or two more fatiguing days than usual we traversed a
glacier pass between two beautiful snow-peaks situated
at a considerable elevation on the Southern face of the
Gross Glockner. It was a difficult walk of twelve or
thirteen hours ; on that occasion we had apparently
thought it due to our self-respect to carry our knapsacks
on our own shoulders ; and the provisions which we
had brought from the miserable lodging, where we had
passed the previous night, consisted of garlicked meat,
and rye-bread flavoured with carraway seeds. Montagu
Butler fell ill, and soon became very ill indeed ; and,
gallantly as he bore himself, I was greatly relieved when
we reached our destination at Pregarten. There was no
inn in the village, and we were directed to the house of
the Parish Priest, whom we found an amiable, a generous,
and a most agreeable host. We had no modern language
in common with him, and were reduced to fall back
upon our Latin. It was a curious illustration of the

necessity for frequent and continuous practice in the speaking of a foreign tongue. Butler was a scholar of ten thousand, whose speciality was the ease and abundance with which he composed in Latin; and yet he was slow and embarrassed in his effort to talk it, whereas our interlocutor rattled away without hesitating for a word, or fumbling over a sentence.

The good Priest could not have entertained us more royally if we had been a couple of young Archdukes, playing truant among the mountains from the Court life at Vienna. He must have cheered and warmed us with mulled wine in our weary and bedraggled plight; for I remember some mild joking about ' Vinum conditum '—as to whether the middle syllable of ' conditum ' was, in this case, to be pronounced long, or short [1]—with a grateful assurance on our part that the wine which he had set before us deserved both the one epithet and the other. Next day, when we were in a condition to enjoy it, he gave us an excellent dinner of four courses, every item of which I can bring back to my memory at this hour. With his command over our only medium of communication our host was able to turn the dialogue into any channel that he wished. Almost the first question that he asked us was whether the Governor-General of British India really and truly drew a salary of three hundred thousand gulden a year; and he employed what apparently was the one English word in his vocabulary by telling us, like a good Austrian, that Lord Palmerston was a ' Firebrand.' He kept us under his roof for three nights until Butler was quite himself again; and he displayed much unwillingness to part with us even then—a compliment my share in which I silently made over to my companion. Montagu Butler's genial familiarity wrought in this case the same

---

[1] Vinum condĭtum = wine stored in the cellar. Vinum condītum = mulled wine.

rapid effect which it very seldom failed to exercise. The
old man seized an opportunity for getting me alone in
the summer-house of his garden, where he examined me
about my friend's parentage and antecedents, and (with
still greater particularity), about his future. I inscribed
an answer, in somewhat awkward Latin, on the fly-leaf
of my pocket Virgil, which concluded by informing him
that my comrade was journeying eastward on a visit to
the Holy Land, from which he would return home to
become a Clergyman of the Church of England. Roman
Catholic as he was, he took from me my book and pencil,
and wrote beneath my last sentence the words :
' Perbene ! Dominus cum ipso ! ' At the end of our
fortnight of separate travel we rejoined the ladies, who
had been waiting for us at the Baths of Ischl ; and not
long afterwards we parted company—Montagu Butler
starting on his road to Greece, and Palestine, and Italy ;
and we for England. We still looked forward to the
prospect of a good time on our way home ; for we were
to meet Macaulay at Paris ; and we knew, from the
experience of a golden week in the near past, what
meeting Macaulay at Paris meant. He received us in
a large and comfortable Salon in the old hotel Wagram,
which looked across the Rue de Rivoli on to the massive
gilt railings of the Tuileries garden. He was in joyous
spirits, brimming over with welcome, and with a piece
of news which he insisted on our guessing. His old
friend Palmerston had offered him a Peerage, and he
had accepted it amidst what may fairly be described as
a general rejoicing on the part of his countrymen.
Henceforward (he told us) we should have to address
him in our letters, after the fashion prevailing in the
seventeenth century, as ' Right Honourable my Singular
Good Lord.'

This walking tour proved the beginning of a
close friendship that was ended only by the death

of the older man in 1918.[1] The warm-hearted interest which Butler took in all that concerned his friends and their families and fortunes, and the charm of the letters in which he expressed that interest when distance intervened, were among the qualities that made him more beloved the older he grew. In 1859, at the early age of twenty-six, he went to his first great post as Head Master of Harrow. The affection and admiration with which my father already then regarded him gives point to a sentence in the following letter written to their common friend Lee Warner in 1862 :

I came up to London [writes my father] with two Harrow boys, who had to be back by 7 o'clock, and were in a fearful stew. They boasted that they had killed respectively 15 and 17 brace that day, which will have grown into 30 and 40 by the time they get to Harrow. At Peterboro' one told me in confidence that the other was a notorious liar ! They always called *him* ' that brute Butler.' They told me there was a jump at Harrow called ' Trevelyan's jump,' which was attributed to me. It was actually done by my cousin. ' Some say there are 50 Herculeses ; others are of opinion there were 100 ' (' Lemprière's Classical Dictionary ').

----

[1] My father used to say that Montagu Butler's notorious objection to smoking was not due to personal idiosyncrasy but to the fact that he was brought up at the close of a generation which had been taught to regard smoking as ungentlemanly. My father's own generation, which included Henry Jackson, had no such tradition. Calverley's *Ode to Tobacco* registers the moment when views on the matter were changing, not without dispute. The bowl of the pipe, lurking half hid under the laurels in the relief on the base of Tennyson's statue in Trinity College ante-chapel, was put there by a secret conspiracy between the sculptor and the donor of the statue, without the knowledge of the master, Montagu Butler. Did he ever discover it ? He never spoke of it.

One recollection of his schoolboy days was contributed by him, in the last years of his life, to the pages of the *Saturday Review* :

I have read an extremely interesting article by A. A. B., in the *Saturday Review*, in which my name is mentioned in connexion with Disraeli's Great Speech on his 1852 Budget. I suppose that I am the only human being alive who heard Mr. Disraeli's marvellous oration ; for I had an opportunity, and a privilege, such as were granted to few. In those days there were three benches for the accommodation of strangers, under the Gallery of the House of Commons, directly facing the Speaker's chair. Whenever the Budget was under discussion, the Permanent Assistant Secretary of the Treasury sat on the back bench to the left of the door of the House, so as to be ready for the aides-de-camp, whom the Chancellor of the Exchequer might despatch to him for information upon any point that arose in debate. The Harrow Christmas holidays had already begun ; and my father brought me into the House with him, as a boy of fourteen, and kept me at his side through the whole of the proceedings, somewhat awed and occasionally bored, but not unfrequently greatly amused and fascinated.

Mr. Disraeli's reply was a unique, an inimitable, and (for anyone who did not hear it) an inconceivable masterpiece. Bristling with points, blazing with fierce and fiery outbursts of rhetoric, and all alive with an inexhaustible profusion of epigrams and sarcasms, it was intelligible and comprehensible to the multitude of hearers who listened to it eagerly for two, or three, hours after midnight had sounded, and who were sorry when the speech was over. It was a revival of the artful and daring eloquence by which, six or seven years before, Sir Robert Peel's followers were tempted and frightened away from their allegiance.

At three in the morning of December 17, Mr. Disraeli resumed his seat, and Mr. Gladstone, looking singularly lithe, active, young, and handsome, ' bounded on to the floor amid a storm of cheering and counter-cheering such as the walls of Parliament have never re-echoed since, and plunged straight into the heart of an oration which, in one hour, doubled his influence in the Commons, and his popularity in the country.' The Conservative members took his intervention very ill, and with some reason ; for at that time there was a generally accepted understanding that the Leader of the House had a vested right to the last word. I understood little of Mr. Gladstone's reply, and did not much care to listen. In that respect my feeling was shared by at least one other person. On the seat immediately beneath us, within two feet of me, sat the Prime Minister [Lord Derby], who had come down to hear how his Chancellor of the Exchequer would acquit himself, and to learn the destiny of his Government. After Mr. Gladstone had at last secured a quiet hearing, and had spoken for five or ten minutes, Lord Derby put his head down upon his folded arms, audibly pronounced the monosyllable ' Dull ! ' and appeared to slumber soundly until the fatal Division was called.

One more reminiscence of my father's childhood recurs to me. I suppose it dates back to 1843 or thereabout. His uncle told him that he was going to spend five more years collecting material to write a History of England. The little boy thought he meant to spend five years buying the very best pens and plenty of blue and white foolscap paper.

CHAPTER II

CAMBRIDGE

In October 1857 my father went up to Cambridge, like a man entering into an inheritance. Never was anyone more eager or better fitted to make the most of the University life of his day. Ever since he was a child, his uncle had been talking to him about Trinity, as the wide, open field of friendship, freedom, work and youthful laurels. From the same source he had learned, before ever he was a freshman, more of the history and traditions of the College from the time of Bentley onwards, than was known to many inhabitants of the Great Court. All his life long he felt towards Trinity as an Athenian towards Athens.

Indeed for the purposes of the author of *The Cambridge Dionysia* and *Horace at Athens* the society of Cambridge and Trinity had then some resemblances to the city of Aristophanes. It was a self-contained republic, of high average intelligence, inclined to look upon the rest of the world as ' Bœotian,' small enough in size to understand a poet's familiar personal allusions, but interesting and important enough to escape provincialism, and to give scope and inspiration to its local bard. Moreover there was then an intellectual unity in Cambridge that has since been dissipated among innumerable triposes and studies. Half the able men were engaged in the intensive study of the classics, and many even of the mathematicians had some classical knowledge. Extreme familiarity with the ancient writers was ' in widest commonalty spread,' and in the best reading sets of the University the study of the classics was humanised by a love of English poetry, letters and history, regarded with a corresponding reverence as the other great achievement of the human race. In this respect the Trinity of Tennyson and Arthur Hallam had changed but little in thirty years. In the twentieth century, the variety of modern studies has put great difficulties in the way of an allusive literature : modern undergraduates share no mental equipment in common.

If there was more intellectual unity in the Cambridge of that day than of our own, there was greater social unity in Trinity than in some other Colleges of that time ; the fashionable, athletic and reading men were not segregated groups. My father, like Pendennis of Boniface, lived among all three, though unlike ' poor Pen ' he was pre-eminently a reading man. Furthermore Trinity drew to itself a larger proportion of the best men of the University than it does under the better distribution of the present age. My father's Cambridge friends, Jebb, the Sidgwicks, Edward Bowen, Henry Jackson, George Young,

Yates Thompson, were all Trinity men, each in some respect very remarkable, none of them mere specialists or mere intellectuals, but alive to life, and eminently suited both to stimulate and correct the quality of intellectual high spirits, which was my father's greatest asset as a young man and as a young author.

During my father's first freshman's term, his uncle noted in his private journal :

I am anxious about George. He has spoken at the Union with éclat. He is fêted and asked to parties and is wild with spirits. I am afraid that he may neglect solid acquirements for showy trifles. I shall see him on Monday and give him some advice.

Affectionate anxiety had betrayed Macaulay into placing two French words in two successive English sentences, contrary to his own rule and custom.

A University magazine called *The Lion*, written by some Trinity men of more literary ambition than scholarship or judgment, appeared in May 1858 ; the introduction talked of ' the pictured page of Livy,' and declared that ' Combined we require but a που στω to move the Universe ' ; there was a poem on 'Lord St. Clair,' which reads like a caricature of Tennyson in his flabbiest mood, but was meant for a masterpiece of romance. Such ' highbrow' effusions are for ever appearing and perishing, each in the latest language of the changing hour. But *The Lion* had no chance, for my father chose it as his butt. First appeared *The Bear*, in form like

D

unto *The Lion*, and sadly mauled its predecessor. Next followed *The Cambridge Dionysia*, an Aristophanic play with the unfortunate authors of *The Lion* as its victims. It was the earliest of his *Juvenilia* that my father thought worthy of reprinting, and it continued to be sold and read almost up to the time of his death. As it is not likely to be printed again in our less classical age, I have appended it to this little book. It will give some idea of my father as an undergraduate at the age of twenty, some idea of the Trinity of that day, and, if the reader be unacquainted with Greek, a glimmering of the spirit of Aristophanes.[1]

At this time of life my father, though eminently popular and moving everywhere amid a cohort of friends, had not that invariable courtesy that marked his conversation later in life, nor experience enough of the world to be always modest or always just. And, indeed, to imitate the true spirit of Aristophanes one cannot afford to be always just. But my father was a young man capable of learning : among the scanty memorials of his youth which he troubled to preserve are several letters of remonstrance addressed to him, severe enough in tone, which he kept because he profited by them. One such plea, from his friend Gerard Cobb, on behalf of the authors of *The Lion*, is a credit both to the man who wrote it and to the man who took it in good part. The result of Cobb's letter was that two emendations were made in the later editions of

---

[1] P. 198, below.

The Cambridge Dionysia, which all must admit to be the removal of blots :

> When an ass
> Of the lowest class
> Talks of ' the pictured page of Livy,'

was altered to

> When a man
> Who can hardly scan
> Talks of ' the pictured page of Livy.'

More remarkable still is the alteration in the first lines of the Parabasis, which originally ran thus :

We wish to praise our poet, who despising fame and pelf
Flew like a bull-dog at the throat of the jagged toothed
    monster itself, [*The Lion*]
Which rages over all the town, from Magdalene-bridge
    to Downing,
With the head of a Lion, and feet of a goose and the ears
    of Robert Browning.

The last line was altered to :

With the bray of a dreamy German ass 'neath the hide
    of Robert Browning.

This very considerable emendation marks not only the heed my father paid to Cobb's remonstrance, but the complete change in his own attitude to Robert Browning, about whom in 1858 he knew no more than Aristophanes knew of Socrates, but whom after 1860 he read and admired more than any other modern poet.

He also preserved a similar remonstrance from his mother against an article which he had written, making fun of Harriet Beecher Stowe's ' Dred, a

Tale of the Dreadful Swamp.' That work had followed on 'Uncle Tom's Cabin,' and sold ' 100,000 copies in four weeks in Great Britain.' The letter, which was taken to heart like all else that his mother said to him at any time of life, must, I think, have been written while he was still at Harrow : it is undated, but ' Dred ' appeared in 1856.

My dearest George,
    It is very seldom I have to find fault with you, but I really have been much vexed by your article on ' Dred.' I do not mean whether it is a good book or not, but it was written by a woman burning with a holy zeal for a cause which is really a very noble one ; tho' I do not think she acts wisely, yet it is the cause of God, and I should be sorry to throw a feather's weight into the opposite scale, which is the cause of the Evil one.   Then it is particularly ungraceful in anyone of your grand-father's [Zachary Macaulay's] descendants to speak disrespectfully of any Antislavery exertions.   I feel that many who really love you, James Cropper in especial, and the Buxtons would be really quite cut to the heart at reading that article.   Then there is another objection which perhaps I should not have felt so strongly but that Tom pointed it out.   No man should ever write of a woman but with a tone of respect and gentleness. There is a sort of chivalrous feeling about a true gentle-man which must complete his character.   I do not like the book and should never object to saying so, but when one thinks how aweful is the evil she contends against, one would rather bid her God speed, than do anything to injure her.   Nothing can be done now, but to say nothing about the authorship to anyone.   Tom says Croker ruined himself completely by his violent way of reviewing Lady Morgan.   He is very anxious you should train yourself to a very courteous tone towards women.

Nevertheless, it is on record that, in the confidence of private conversation, ' Tom ' was capable of poking rather rude fun at the pretensions of Harriet Beecher Stowe, though he always obeyed his own rule in ' writing of a woman.'

While my father was enjoying every side of undergraduate life, and was ' commencing author ' at the expense of the unhappy *Lion*, he did not neglect his proper work for the Tripos, the ultimate academic ordeal when ' the man is weighed as in a balance.' In those days each candidate was placed in individual order of merit. And the excitement about the results of the Classical and the Mathematical Triposes was all the more intense as there were then only those two lists that counted, the Moral and Physical Science Schools being in their merest infancy, and there being no other ' fancy Triposes ' such as History, Law or Modern Languages. Personal and corporate rivalries ran the higher in the field of scholarship, because athletic competition was not yet organised and advertised in the modern fashion, and Colleges still cared almost as much about their successes in the Tripos as about their places on the river.

So he read with zeal ; but he read alone, and did not, until late in his third year, go to any ' private coach,' although it was regarded as essential even for the best men to secure the services of Shilleto, if they would do themselves justice in the examination room. The place then occupied in University life by the ' private coach ' was due to the fact that Fellows of Colleges were content merely to lecture, and did not, as now, recognise it as part of their duty to ' supervise ' the individual studies of the undergraduates. My father's peculiar resolve to dispense with Shilleto's aid was due, like so much else in his early life, to the desire to imitate and to please his uncle. When Macaulay was an undergraduate, the great days of the ' private coach ' had not begun, and the following passage from one of his last letters to Ellis throws a curious light on the change in Cambridge methods of classical reading between 1819 and 1859.

We have very good accounts of George from various quarters. He did very well at the University Scholarship examination. No Trinity man of his year was near him. One man of his own year, a Johnian, was above him ; and another, a Kingsman, close upon him. But this looks promising for a high place in the Classical Tripos. The examiners say too that he is very greatly improved. I cannot help feeling pleased that this improvement should have been the effect purely of his own unassisted studies, carried on from love of ancient literature. He has had no cramming, but has gone in against the pupils of Donaldson and Shilleto with no other training than that which you and I had. I have half a mind to take the responsibility of advising him to go on in the same way during the next twenty months ; and he would certainly take my advice : for he has struggled obstinately against the prevailing fashion, and has set his heart, as he owned to his mother, on being a scholar after the pattern of our generation, and not after the new mode. His natural feeling about me has done him some harm, with, I hope, some good. His neglect of Mathematics is to be ascribed to the bad example which I set him.[1] It is owing to me too, I must say on the other side, that he lives in an atmosphere reeking with Carlylism, Ruskinism, Browningism, and other equally noxious isms, without the slightest taint of the morbific virus.

In view of this letter, written in April 1859, I cannot help feeling that Macaulay's death in the following Christmas was not an unmixed catastrophe to his nephew. It set him free from the burden of his own too loyal heart. In 1860 he studied with Shilleto, and won the second place in the Classical Tripos of 1861, being beaten by Abbott of John's alone. At the same time he caught the three diseases of Browningism, Ruskinism and Carlylism, and never recovered.

Shilleto, the coach, being married, could not be a Fellow. But he was a great scholar—of Porson's school in more respects than one. If ever 'cramming' can improve men's minds, the minds of Shilleto's pupils were improved. Something of the character and humour of this remarkable man, something also of my father as an undergraduate, may be gleaned from these notes which Shilleto wrote him, and which he religiously preserved, though he destroyed or lost nearly all his other Cambridge correspondence. Evidently he had at last applied to Shilleto to take him as a pupil

[1] In 1905 my father wrote to Montagu Butler about the proposed abolition of Greek as a compulsory subject in the Cambridge Entrance Examination: ' I love Greek too much to desire anyone to hate it as I hated mathematics.'

though in his third year, and at first without success :

24 Trumpington Street,
Cambridge.
February 22, 1860.

Sir,

Sidgwick tells me that you are desirous to become my pupil during the next Term, and that you have personally applied to me. I do not ordinarily ask the names of applicants for whom I have not room. Known to me by reputation but not personally, I was unable to state to you orally what I now say literally. My coach is full both outside and inside, and, having no connection with the respectable party which started the omnibus, I regret that I cannot engage an extra conveyance. I am afraid therefore that I shall not have the honour of snubbing you or of incurring your dislike.

. I have the honour to be,
Sir,
Your very obedient Servant,
RICHARD SHILLETO.

But five days later Shilleto relents :

February 27, 1860.

My dear Sir,

I have misgivings as to the establishment of a bad precedent, but if Sidgwick has told you so (and being a brother Yorkshireman and a West Ridinger to boot I cannot but believe that he speaks truth) I am afraid that after all I *am* doomed to snub you.

Yours very truly,
RICHARD SHILLETO.

April 2, 1860.

My dear Trevelyan,

I have not a very good spare hour on Thursday, and—you wretch—Friday is Good Friday. Can we compromise? Will you come on Thursday evening, and, if you have such strange tastes, take a cup of tea? It will undoubtedly be followed by a Tankard if not of Audit at least of Guinness.

Yours ever most truly,
RICHARD SHILLETO.

May 2.

My dear Trevelyan,

I write to you in sorrow not in anger. Do let me seriously expostulate. I am really serious. Why play the fool with me and—what's worse—with yourself? You told me this morning you would do the Composition in my ante-room—I look in about five minutes after you leave me and you are gone.[1] What does this mean? I will be determined. If you will not work I must cut the concern altogether. I dined in Trinity yesterday. I told Mathison of your delict. He only shrugged his shoulders. The Public Orator was opposite me—'We have all tried what we can do, but have done no good.' I make a final appeal to your good sense. Come tomorrow with work whatever it is. Let me have some Composition.

Yours ever most truly,
RICHARD SHILLETO.

In another undated letter is a humorous remonstrance : it would seem that my father had accidentally addressed a letter to his coach leaving out the ' h ' of his name, thereby rendering it, in sound at least, no other than ' silly toe.'

My dear Trevelyan,

The ' misnomer ' is not new. I was dubbed so (I believe) by our present grandest of Orators. When my

---

[1] Oral tradition at Cambridge has it that Shilleto had locked the outer door of his ante-room and pocketed the key, so as to keep my father there, and that the truant climbed down out of the window. Unfortunately I only heard this too late to ask my father if it were true. It is not unlikely, for Shilleto was an eccentric man.

ἠθικοφυσικόληροι came out, a copy was shewn me pencilled ἀνώνομον λέγεται δὲ Μωροδακτύλου.[1] Likewise Thompson, that now is Professor, wrote me a note of invitation to dine in Hall on the πιθοιγία [Audit Feast], his note bearing date 1 Nov. 1848, asking withal for a copy of a Fragment of M[orodactulo]s. I bear in mind this (having it also recorded in a Diary which I kept then) for it was the first time in my M.A. life that I on that day dined in Trinity. For future builders or repairers of the Greek Theatre I add that I find (on reference to the said Diary) that the Ale was sweet and not so potent as to make me cut the preps of the evening. Still it is not recorded that I poured any on the ground.

Look to this Right Reverend G. Otto Troveliar, Particular Baptist Minister, &c., &c., &c.

I don't expose you outsidely to ' The middle finger and the Postman's scorn ' as you did ' Silleto,' you abominable——

Please forgive

Yours most truly,

RICHARD SHILLETO.[2]

So Shilleto saw my father well through the Tripos. But although he had deigned in the end to take the coach, he realised none the less Macaulay's ideal of the independent scholar, as one who ' read Plato with his feet on the fender.' All through his long life, and particularly during the last fourteen years of it, after he had given up any other intellectual task, he read and reread the

---

[1] ' Anonymous, but it is said to be Silly Toe's ' (Silleto's).

[2] The reference in this letter to the πιθοιγία as the Trinity Audit Feast, and the words 'it is not recorded that I poured any on the ground,' are explained by passages in my father's *Cambridge Dionysia*, where ' Shillibere ' is of course Shilleto (see pp. 201, 204 below). Shilleto must have been quite familiar with that piece which had appeared about two years before this letter was written.

classical authors, from the most famous down to the latest and most obscure. His friend Henry Jackson, Professor of Greek at Cambridge, used always to say that my father read far more of the classics for pleasure than he himself or any other professional. He seemed to us to be for ever reading the Greek dramatists, Thucydides and Livy. And he brought to the perusal of Cicero's letters the same affectionate intimacy with the personalities of that great period of history which he felt for the not wholly dissimilar aristocrats and politicians whose social life he has pictured in the ' Early History of Charles James Fox.'

The last letters that were exchanged between Macaulay and his nephew, in the winter of the historian's death, are not without interest :

Holly Lodge,
Kensington.
Oct. 24, 1859.

Dear George,

I take the liberty to point out to you a false spelling of which you are guilty, a false spelling, too, particularly censurable in a scholar—' to *pander* to the insatiable love of rhetoric.' Now you are surely aware that the word *pandar* is simply the proper name of the warrior whom Homer calls Pandarus, and who is prompted by Minerva to break the treaty between the Greeks and Trojans. The poets and romancers of the middle ages, knowing generally that he had been represented by Homer as a faithless and dishonorable man, made him connive, and more than connive, at the gallantries of his niece Cressida. Thence the name Pandarus or Pandar was given to pimps. When Falstaff wishes Pistol to carry a love-letter to a married woman, Pistol exclaims ' Shall I

Sir Pandarus of Troy become?' It is therefore most incorrect to spell the word *pander*.[1] In fact this spelling, like *Syren*, like *Sybil*, like *pigmy*, and some other spellings which might be mentioned, raises a strong presumption that the person who is guilty of it does not know Greek.

I am glad that you are properly interested about the siege of Syracuse. The Seventh Book of Thucydides is the finest piece of history in the world. Livy, Tacitus, Sallust, Xenophon vanish before it. It is absolutely perfect. I have often wished to visit Syracuse. But I believe that the coast has undergone considerable changes. The quarries in which the prisoners were confined remain ; and to judge by the pictures which I have seen, must be well worth visiting.[2]

I wonder that you should carry away from the *De Natura Deorum* no impression but that of the style. Surely the Academic philosopher makes mincemeat of the Epicurean. The first book I think the best. But on the whole I prefer the argument against the Epicurean in the *De Finibus*. The *De Fato* and the *De Divinatione* are also, I think, excellently reasoned.

I have of late been reading Bentley's ' Horace ' again, with frequent dissent, with frequent doubt, and with constant admiration. I am meditating an attack on Athenaeus, of whom I know less than I could wish.

Mamma [Lady Trevelyan] came back on Thursday. On Friday she and Alice dine with me ; and to-morrow I am to dine with them. I am well enough in body— very much otherwise, as you may suppose, in mind.

[1] Macaulay's history of the word is correct, but high authority can be found for my father's spelling of it.
[2] When Secretary of the Admiralty my father visited Syracuse in a British gunboat. He used to express regret that it could not have been present at the battle in the bay, to turn the scales of history in favour of the Athenian fleet. A line of old quarry near Greenleighton on his Wallington estate used always to be called by us *Epipolæ*, after a fancied resemblance that he saw in it to the heights over which the hoplites were driven in the land battle.

But I put a force on myself and plague other people with my feelings as little as I can.

Ever yours,

MACAULAY.

The depression of spirits to which he refers, in so far as it was not really physical, was caused by the approaching departure of his sister from England. In January 1859 Sir Charles Trevelyan had been appointed Governor of Madras and had sailed in the following month to take up his duties there—his last words to Macaulay being ' You have always been a most kind brother to me.' Lady Trevelyan was shortly to follow him, but she remained in England nearly a year because of her brother's condition. His ill health made him less well able to support a separation from his sister which he felt would be final. But the kind Gods so disposed that he never knew the misery of living far from her care.

The last letter that Macaulay received from my father was found on his writing table at his death ; it refers to the part taken by Cambridge University in the national Volunteer movement which the fear of Napoleon III had inspired.

Nov. 21, 1859.

Dearest Uncle,

Amongst all the wars and rumours of wars it is not very easy to keep one's head empty for the reception of Latin and Greek. I must do my best to enlist your sympathies in the cause of our wretched rifle-corps. We have between 400 and 500 names enrolled ; we have elected our officers, separated our men into companies, and shown a bright example of patriotism to the youth of England. Thus much we have done for ourselves, but some nemesis pursues us. We are bullied and slighted by all the powers that are : the Lord Lieutenant refuses us commissions, because we have not chosen the young lords as officers : the Vice-Chancellor's applications in our behalf are sent unopened from the Secretary at War to the Commander-in-Chief, and back from the Commander-in-Chief to the Secretary at War. We ask the militia to give us drill sergeants, and are required to show an order from the Lord Lieutenant : we engage recruiting sergeants from the town, and humbly request leave of the Master [Whewell, of Trinity] to use the ground at the back of the College, and receive an ignominious refusal. One would think we were members of a Phœnix Club, rather than honest undergraduates, burning with zeal for every jot and tittle of Queen, Church and State. There is a report that Cobden has come from a visit to France, and is exhorting the Manchester men to arm ! [Not confirmed by history.]

You must not think, however, that the misfortunes of our rifle-corps distract my attention to any great extent from Cicero and Plato. The Athenian philosophers were disputing poker and tongs while the Spartan army was ravaging Attica ; and I have not the least doubt but that Socrates managed to find some fellow citizen in the retreat from Delium who was willing to undergo, then and there, a cross examination about the Beautiful and the True for the sake of the protection of the most hardy hoplite of Athens.

It is most satisfactory about the election of Butler as Head Master of Harrow. We celebrated it by an extemporary symposium in the middle of the New Court, giving claret to everyone, whether an Harrovian or not, who was willing to rejoice with us. It was an honour to human nature, the amount of sympathy we obtained.

LORD MACAULAY

In the last year of his life.

There is a report of your two next volumes being on the eve of publication. It is pleasant to look forward to a month or six weeks of union at Christmas. We shall have much to tell, hear and arrange.

Ever your affecte. nephew,

G. O. TREVELYAN.

Macaulay replied in the last letter he ever wrote to his nephew (now exhibited in the Fitzwilliam Museum):

Holly Lodge,
Nov. 22, 1859.

Dear George,

Thanks for your letter. This is the day of the Christening,[1] and the hour of the Christening; and I am writing to you instead of doing my duty at the font. The reason is that the ninth plague of Egypt is upon us. The fog is such that I cannot see one tree in my garden; and, bad as things are here, the postman reports that they are worse still at Knightsbridge. If I were to venture out, we should probably have a burial in the family, as well as a christening. I therefore stay, very disconsolately, by my fire side, and wait for my footman whom I have sent to Belgravia for news, and who may perhaps find his way back through the darkness in the course of a few hours.

I am glad that you mean to pass the Christmas vacation at home. But you must read resolutely. There is no chance of my visiting Cambridge at present. The story about my two volumes is a newspaper lie. One volume may perhaps appear two years hence.

I sympathise with the grievances of your rifle corps. But there is nothing new under the sun. The young volunteers of 1803, of whom few are now left, and these few Law Lords, Archdeacons, and Professors, were treated in just the same way. My old master Preston

---

[1] Of Henry Holland, son of his niece Margaret.

was one of them, and retained many years a bitter sense
of the injustice and incivility which they had to endure.
By the bye, one of the most eager and warlike among
them was Garratt, the second wrangler and first Smith's
prize man of 1804. This always amused me : for
Garratt was quite a dwarf, the very smallest man that
I ever saw gratis.

I was delighted by Butler's success ; and the more so
because it was unexpected. I suppose that he will be
made a Doctor of Divinity without delay. My kind
regards to him if he is at Cambridge, and my warm
congratulations.

Sir Charles Wood, the Secretary of State for India,
dined here on Saturday. I was glad to learn from him
that your father is going on as well as possible, and
giving the highest satisfaction to the home authorities.

Ellis told me that he had heard from you. I am of
his mind about the Parmenides and about the two
dialogues which cannot be separated from the Parmenides, the Politicus and the Sophista. Whewell agrees
with us. But he thinks the Laches genuine ; and I am
sure it is spurious. I will give you my reasons at
Christmas if you care to hear them.

If you are asked to write the tripos verses of 1860,
you may make an excellent eclogue on the Cambridge
Rifle Corps. Menalcas with his bow and quiver, comes
to the mouth of a cave overhung with ivy and wild vines,
where Daphnis and Alexis are contending in verse, with
Damoetas for judge. Menalcas indignantly bids them
throw away their pipes, and take to their arms. ' Have
you not heard that the tyrant who calls himself a
Heracleid,[1] threatens Arcadia with invasion and sub-
jugation ? All the shepherds are mustering from
Cyllene to Phigaleia. The beacons are ready to be
lighted on the tops of Maenalus and Parthenius. The
women and children are taking refuge behind the walls

---

[1] Napoleon III.

of Tegea and Orchomenus. There are mighty gather-
ings of archers and spearmen in the valleys of Ladon
and Erymanthus. And you sit here disputing the prize
of singing (*i.e.* the Craven scholarship) as if all were
quiet.' Perhaps you might bring in a fling at the Lord
Lieutenant.

Ever yours,

MACAULAY.

The account of his uncle's death which my
father gave in the biography is so relative to his
own life that I reprint it here without apology :

In a contemporary account of Macaulay's last illness
it is related that on the morning of Wednesday, the
28th of December [1859], he mustered strength to dictate
a letter addressed to a poor curate, enclosing twenty-five
pounds ; after signing which letter he never wrote his
name again. Late in the afternoon of the same day I
called at Holly Lodge, intending to propose myself to
dinner ; an intention which was abandoned as soon as
I entered the library. My uncle was sitting, with his
head bent forward on his chest, in a languid and drowsy
reverie. The first number of the *Cornhill Magazine* lay
unheeded before him, open at the first page of
Thackeray's story of Lovel the Widower. He did not
utter a word, except in answer ; and the only one of
my observations that at this distance of time I can recall
suggested to him painful and pathetic reflections, which
altogether destroyed his self-command.

On hearing my report of his state, my mother resolved
to spend the night at Holly Lodge. She had just left
the drawing-room to make her preparations for the visit
when a servant arrived with an urgent summons. As
we drove up to the porch of my uncle's house, the maids
ran crying out into the darkness to meet us, and we

E

knew that all was over. We found him in the library,
seated in his easy chair, and dressed as usual ; with his
book on the table beside him, still open at the same
page. . . . He died as he had always wished to die ;—
without pain ; without any formal farewell ; preceding
to the grave all whom he loved ; and leaving behind
him a great and honourable name, and the memory of
a life every action of which was as clear and transparent
as one of his own sentences.

My poor grandmother had scarcely seen her
brother's body laid at the foot of Addison's statue
in the Abbey before she hurried out to India, to
find herself there involved in the chief catastrophe
of her husband's life. In all respects save one, Sir
Charles Trevelyan's administration of Madras had
been particularly successful. But he had differed
from the Government at Calcutta on a point of
financial policy for all India ; in March 1860 he and
his Council had recorded in a minute their difference of opinion from the Governor-General and his
Council. My grandfather believed that the case
thus put forward by Madras was not given a
hearing in the Legislative Council, and therefore,
on his sole responsibility, made public the Madras
Council's minute of protest. This was a breach
of administrative custom and propriety astonishing
in so experienced a public servant. My father
used always to say that if his mother had been in
India at the time, the minute would never have
been published. But she arrived to find the
mischief done. Her husband's impetuous zeal
had not on this occasion, as on so many others,

been restrained by her calmness and good sense.[1]

The discipline of the service demanded his recall. It was effected in May 1860, by one of his oldest friends and admirers, Sir Charles Wood, who took occasion to declare in public official documents that Trevelyan's administration of Madras had, in all other respects, been of the greatest service. His temporary disgrace was followed two years later by a remarkable triumph when Wood and Palmerston sent him out to Calcutta as Financial Member of Council, because the financial views that he had so unwisely made public were found to have been just. His private letters seem to indicate that he never repented of the action that cost him so dear, but which, in his opinion, led to the ultimate triumph of his policy.

But the year 1860 was a black one for my grandparents, returning together to England under a cloud, with no brother Tom waiting to welcome and console them. My father felt all these things deeply ; but the spirits of youth recover soon, or it would be a sad world. In the winter of 1860-1 he was working full blast for his Tripos [2]—that is

[1] Macaulay had written in his private journal, June 5, 1859 (about half a year before his own death, and not quite a year before my grandfather's recall) : ' As Hannah justly says, Trevelyan has all his life been saying and doing rash things, and yet has always got out of his scrapes.' The pitcher went once too often to the well.

In 1912 my father wrote to my brother Robert : ' I remember going down with my father to Southampton in the early months of 1859, when he was leaving England for India, and watching the P. and O. liner getting dim in the distance. Ah me ! What an avoidable catastrophe it was. People should always beware of the governing impulse in their character.'

[2] In those days the Tripos examination was held in January, normally in a candidate's eleventh term.

to say, as hard as a human being can work and keep his health. Though no athlete, he always took vigorous exercise, and sometimes the exercise seems to have been very vigorous indeed. The winter of his Tripos was the first and I think the only period of his life that he ever hunted, and apparently it was under pressure from the Prince of Wales, then a Trinity undergraduate, resident at Madingley Hall, three miles away.

My dear Mother,

Yesterday, as I was washing preparatory to rackets, there came a knock at the door, and I issued from my bedroom, covered with soap and in my shirtsleeves, full in the face of the Prince. He stayed about a quarter of an hour, talked a great deal about the pictures on the walls, etc., and then began to abuse the men up here for not hunting. He reiterated the wish he had expressed on Sunday about my hunting, so, as the royal desires jumped with mine, I am going out for the first time on Friday, and have been providing boots, cords, etc., in a great hurry. A day's hunting will be the very thing, and just relieve one's mind for a day from the vexation of the coming examination. It certainly would be rather awkward to break a collar-bone just now.

Dear Mother,   Saturday.

I write to relieve your mind. We had a wonderful day of it. Eleven hours in the saddle. Out of a field of more than 300 only twelve or fifteen were in at the end. We had a run of an hour after four in the afternoon. Sir C. Wood's son, Hope Grant, and myself rode with the Prince and had great fun. I was on a strong Cambridge hack, which rushed blindly at everything and gave me two bad falls. The last was rather memorable. My brute caught all its legs in the hedge,

and came down on me on the other side. The Prince
followed, and fell exactly in the same manner, at the
very same place. Conceive my feeling when my future
sovereign rolled on his head at my feet. I am all right,
with the exception of a great bruise in the back, where
my horse came on me. It was a severe ordeal for the
first day's hunting. It has done me a world of good,
and my classics present a much more pleasing aspect.
I am glad I never hunted before. It is much too
entrancing for a man before his degree. O what will
that degree be?

Dearest Mother,
   The tripos is over. Such a week I never remember.
I went to bed regularly every night at eleven, and fell
asleep every morning regularly at half-past five. The
wear of body and mind was strangely great, but the
excitement kept me up, and enabled me to do more
than during one's healthiest moments. To-morrow I
am going hunting, and have no fear of throwing off all
care. I have been asked again to dinner at Madingley,
and shall therefore be unable to come down till Thursday.

At this stage the College authorities, who had
been generously holding their hand till the
examination was over, intervened and sent him
down ' till degree day, the 21st of March,' because
he had, for a long time past, cut chapel with
extreme regularity. His last words about the
Prince are : ' I liked him better than ever before,
as one cares less about pleasing him. He has been
very attentive and kind about the examination.'
   The Tripos result, in those days arranged in
order of merit, gave Abbott, Trevelyan, Cornish,
Austen-Leigh as the order of the first four.

Fortunately for those concerned Jebb was not in till the next year.

His success in the Tripos of 1861 was followed that same year by the production of *Horace at the University of Athens*. It was first composed for acting, and was first printed by Jonathan Palmer at Cambridge in 1861. Its not too recondite academic fun long remained a favourite among Cambridge men of the old classical school ; it has passed through many editions, of which the reprint at the end of this volume is the latest. But, however popular among the author's contemporaries, it was less highly appreciated by some of those in power. Whewell, as Master of Trinity, considered my father lacking in deference, and was believed to resent such lines as the often-quoted description of the undergraduate dinner in hall :

> We still consume, with mingled shame and grief,
> Veal that is tottering on the verge of beef.[1]

And still more the two couplets :

> The fellowships have gone, save one in three,
> In inverse ratio to the degree.
> And we expect next year a junior op
> Will, by the help of book work, come out top.

Being about to compete for a Fellowship himself, my father felt these lines to be rash, and at the last moment suppressed them. But the thrifty Mr. Palmer strengthened the bindings of the book

[1] My father always acknowledged that he had taken this line from the prose of Coleridge.

by inserting the suppressed page inside the cloth of the cover. My father was not cognizant of this, and regretted it sincerely, but of course everyone supposed that he had given insidious directions to the binder. Copies that I possess contain the concealed offence, easily revealed by tearing open the light cloth binding.

In any case my father failed in his second attempt to obtain a Fellowship in October 1862, and as he had no very high opinion of the scholarship of some of the successful candidates (Jebb also was passed over that year), he decided not to sit again the following October as he might have done. This course was undoubtedly wise, even if partly inspired by pique. To waste another year in keeping up his classics for another of the endless examinations he had been doing ever since he had competed for the Gregory at Harrow, would have been merely to mark time.[1] Wider prospects were opening to him. His father was going out to India once more, as Financial Member of Council, and offered to take him as private secretary. Since his ultimate destiny was certain to lie in the London world of politics and literature, and not in the groves of Academe, since in short he would never have been a don for life, the Fellowship was not essential to him. It would have been the finest feather in the cap of youth, but nothing more.

[1] Fellowships at Trinity are now awarded for dissertations, that is for original work. No one can call such work a waste of time, but in my father's day candidates had to keep their classical or mathematical examination knowledge up to the mark for every annual competition. That was a waste of time indeed for a young man at the beginning of life.

The extent and character of my father's annoyance is portrayed in the following letter, written in the heat :

October 1862.

My dearest father,

I really feel more than I can well express the pain that you are sure to feel when you hear the result of this examination. Neither Jebb nor myself are on the list. None of the examiners pretend to say that we were beaten. If I had been wise I should have taken warning by last time and spared you and myself a periodical humiliation. It is a most cruel thing to call an examination a competition, and then to give the prizes by seniority. Never again will I put my reputation in any hands but my own. Vexatious as it is, I care much more for you and Mamma than myself. The examiners all express themselves thoroughly satisfied with me, which is really adding insult to injury. With great love,

I remain,

Yr. aff. son,

G. O. TREVELYAN.

In his old age, my father wrote on an envelope containing this letter :

I am not ashamed of the letter. After the examination Lady Trevelyan [Pauline, wife of Sir Walter] told me that Dr. Whewell had told her two months beforehand that I must not expect to be elected as 'so many men of the previous year were in.' Under this pre-determination of his, it was a farce, and an insult, to allow Jebb and me to compete.

Jebb, who had been senior classic in the summer of 1862, the year after Abbott's and my father's, was already recognised throughout England as the greatest scholar of the rising generation. It was

Jebb's first chance for a Fellowship, and my
father's second.

His quarrel was not with Trinity, but with
Whewell, its despotic Master. I do not wish to
pronounce whether, as Henry Jackson maintained,
he was unnecessarily angry. At any rate he was
not sulky. He gave what he was pleased to call
a ' non-Fellowship dinner ' to the most jovial of
his friends, in which, *in joco atque vino*, he made a
speech saying he would ' use no Joe-Priori argument '—an allusion which some of the learned will
understand. And so, in a blaze of high spirits,
fun and youthful indignation he vanished from the
place he loved so well, but which could not and
should not in any event have held him back much
longer from the larger world where he was due.

All's well that ends well. My father lost
nothing by leaving Cambridge when he did, and
he appreciated in a very peculiar manner his
election in 1885 to an Honorary Fellowship of
Trinity. His full-length portrait by Frank Holl
now hangs in the Old Combination Room.

Of all his Trinity friends only one survived him,
Sir George Young, who lived to ninety-two.
One episode of their undergraduate life is highly
characteristic of that man of iron. He and my
father set out to walk from Cambridge to London,
starting, with unnecessary zeal, at midnight.
There was a thick fog, and they became in-
cautiously absorbed in a political discussion ;
when the argument came to an end they looked

about them and found they had made a vast circle and were coming back into Trumpington. My father went back to bed, but Sir George Young set out again and walked to London ! It was the same spirit that recently took his son Geoffrey up the Matterhorn on one leg. I may mention that Geoffrey Young and I walked from Cambridge to London when our turn came, but started as comfortably late as five in the morning.

The friendships made at Trinity remained the most intimate of my father's life. His later friendships with political colleagues—Harcourt, Morley, Rosebery and above all Bryce—were very pleasant and sincere, but few of these had the same personal closeness as his feeling for Henry and Arthur Sidgwick, Edward Bowen, Henry Jackson, Montagu Butler, Yates Thompson, Richard Jebb, Sir George Young, and George Howard, afterwards the artist Earl of Carlisle. Most of them were members of the Apostles Society. At that time Henry Sidgwick, with his eager thirst for the impartial truth on all subjects, was its heart and soul. My father, though a more exoteric philosopher, was proud and happy to attend its meetings.

This group of Cambridge friends was not a mutual admiration society ; a society for mutual criticism would be nearer the mark of description. Strong individualists, with nothing in common but the Victorian attitude towards life and morals, and the liberal attitude towards moderate reform usual among young University men of the 'sixties, each carved out his own path in the world towards an ideal chosen by himself, and each spoke his mind freely in criticism of the others without the least danger to friendship. My father's gifts as a young man were such that too easy admiration from his closest College friends would have been very dangerous ; he never got it and he never sought it.

On these terms, his dearest affections of all were given, till death parted them, to Edward Bowen and Henry Sidgwick. The future Harrow Master and author of the words of the immortal Harrow Songs was, as an undergraduate, full of a quaint inventive originality, sometimes degenerating into the Puckish. Bowen not only revived for awhile the Second Trinity Boat, but played many practical jokes of an intellectual order. Once he spread an hour's wild dismay by posting up a bogus Tripos list, ingeniously combining the probable and the fantastic. His unforgettable personality was indeed a blend of apparently incongruous elements of character. The earnest, ascetic follower of duty, formidably stern with himself and others, was not only a poet but a freakish and irresponsible creator of fun. Bowen continued till the end to charm while he puzzled boys and men. He soon ceased to puzzle my father, who accepted him, with all his tricks, as a gift of God.

The deep mutual attachment of Henry Sidgwick and my father was increased, I think, by a consciousness on both sides that each was complementary to the other. In many ways no one could be more different from the author of *Horace at Athens* than the author of *The Methods of Ethics*, the scrupulous, hesitating seeker after the subtleties of truth, with all its 'subintents and saving clauses,' on every subject that concerns man as a reasoning being. But they met on equal terms and there was ground in common. Sidgwick, an excellent literary critic, and a student of history and politics as of all things human, greatly appreciated my father's gifts and shared many of his enthusiasms, though always with an eye widely open on his friend's limitations. Of these he once spoke to me—for I knew him well in his last years—with an earnest desire to warn me of them, since I could not afford to imitate my father's deficiencies without his powers. At bottom their mutual affection was based on moral grounds. Perhaps indeed that is true of all friendship.

In political matters my father and his Cambridge friends were most of their lives in agreement. Then Home Rule came to divide them, though it made no difference to their affection and conversation. The Boer War followed, and the more intimate of his old College friends, Unionist as much as Liberal, disliked the moral atmosphere in which it was initiated and waged. A peculiarly close sympathy therefore united Edward Bowen and Henry Sidgwick to my father at the moment when, in the last year of the century, death took them both from him, as it were at one blow.

At the beginning of Part II of his 'History of
the American Revolution,' 1903, stands this
inscription :

THESE VOLUMES ARE DEDICATED

TO THE BELOVED MEMORY

OF

EDWARD ERNEST BOWEN

AND

HENRY SIDGWICK

---

*'Animæ, quales neque candidiores
Terra tulit, neque queis me sit devinctior alter.*

CHAPTER III

INDIA. PARLIAMENT. POLITICS AND LITERATURE
IN LONDON. MARRIAGE. (1862-1869)

DURING the year and more that my father spent
at Cambridge after his Tripos, he began to take
an increasing interest in public affairs. His New
Year resolutions for 1862, noted in his private
diary, pledge him ' to learn to speak ; to make
an honest effort at political knowledge.' He had
not yet come under the influence of that strong
wave of reforming liberalism that caught hold of
him and his Cambridge friends in the later 'sixties.
His sympathies were with the South rather than
the North at the beginning of the American Civil
War, an opinion of which his repentance was
singularly rapid and complete. But liberal sympathies in European affairs, at the time when the
Kingdom of Italy was being made with all the
romantic circumstance of Garibaldi's adventures,
appealed to him and his friends as inevitably as the
cause of Greece and Byron had appealed to young
Trinity men forty years before. So, when he visited
Paris in 1862, he writes in a letter thence to a friend :

As to the French, I am perfectly satisfied that the only
very strong feeling the nation has on Italian politics is

an intense distaste for the idea of a united Italy. It is a
jealous fear, more than anything else. I saw nothing
but liberals in Paris, and in no single case did I get the
smallest encouragement on the subject. Montalembert
is bitter to the last degree. That, however, you might
expect from his Church views, but everyone, for instance
the whole family of the Duvergiers, are very strong
against Victor Emmanuel. It is considered almost bad
taste to be for Italian unity. People who attack measures
of the Emperor's because they are his, do not abuse him
for retaining Rome but for having helped Piedmont.
As to the journals taking the liberal side, I believe that
it is simply because the Emperor is rather more willing
than any other Frenchman to leave Rome. The general
feeling produced by one's stay in France, on this subject,
was intense disappointment at the real dislike for the
Italian cause everywhere expressed.

A letter to Henry Sidgwick of the same date
gives more of his impressions of French ' liberal '
society under the Empire :

On Monday a lady asked us to dinner to meet Guizot,
Montalembert, Mignet, Jules Simon, a professor *destitué*
for his opinions (every other person is a professor *destitué*
for his opinions), Prévot Paradol, and the other lights of
the unfortunate constitutional party. It was great fun.
Though there were eleven at table, the conversation was
general, perhaps because there was only one lady. It
was just like a Trinity dinner. They abused the
Emperor just as we abuse the Master [Whewell]. After
dinner I had a hot discussion with Montalembert, who
defended the temporal power, and the Bourbon dynasty
of Naples. Eventually he said ' You English are so
inconsequent. You oppress Ireland, etc.' I instantly
said that for my part if the Irish wished to be free, in
Heaven's name let them be so. He said ' You are the

first Englishman I ever met who said that. Come to me on Wednesday.' On Tuesday I was at another liberal salon, where I had a very interesting talk with Odillon Barrot, and where a professor ' *destitué* for his opinions,' read, with closed doors and excluded servants, a satire in verse on *les démolisseurs de Paris*. It was rather dirty like everything French. By the bye, I met Renan the other day. The people here are kind and hospitable to a degree. Nothing strikes me so much as the intense ignorance of the nation on everything that is not French. They know nothing of Germany : and hardly more of England. My firm conviction is that no author of our time is generally known even by name, in French society. The single exception seems to be Macaulay. To be introduced as his nephew, which in England I inexpressibly detest, is a passport here which never fails. The education of the young men is very defective. They leave school at 17, and *font leur droit*, which is what we should call kicking about in Paris. I shall be in Cambridge about the 10th of May and stay on till our reading party. It will be the last time we shall be in residence together and must be proportionately jolly. Your account of [Oscar] Browning is very droll. Yes ! I am a little bored, but I am gaining the habits of application and punctuality which *vous autres* got at Rugby.

In the course of this same year he wrote and published a little extravaganza, in the style of *Horace at Athens*, but dealing with English and Italian politics, called *The Pope and his Patron*. He never thought it worthy of republication, and indeed he did not yet understand the world of politics as well as he understood it four years later, when he wrote the highly successful *Ladies in Parliament*.

At the end of 1862, immediately after he had failed for the Fellowship, he sailed for India, and during the next twelve months acted as private secretary to his father, then Financial Member of Council. His task, though diversified by a certain amount of travel and sport, put him in a much better position than that of an ordinary M.P. on tour, to understand Anglo-Indian administration. The letters that he wrote home describing what he saw and thought were published in *Macmillan's Magazine*, and in 1864 reappeared in book form, under the title of *The Competition Wallah*.[1] The work was equally well received in India and in England, and began my father's literary reputation in the larger world of London, as distinct from the academic successes of *The Cambridge Dionysia* and *Horace*. It did much to inspire Englishmen with an interest in the work of their countrymen in India ; and it still remains the most vivid account of the Anglo-Indian world immediately after the Mutiny. He followed it up in 1865 with ' Cawnpore,' written after his return to England, a striking piece of narrative, his first effort at history proper. In lighter vein was *The Dawk Bungalow ; or Is his Appointment Pucka?* first acted ' at the residence of the Lieutenant-Governor of Bengal, before an audience nine-tenths of which held either pucka or cutcha appointments,' and often since reprinted.

[1] A ' competition wallah ' was the term used to describe an Indian Civil Servant who had got his post by the method of competitive examination, introduced into the Company's service as early as 1853, largely owing to the efforts of my grandfather, the chief advocate, if not the originator of the idea for the Civil Service both in India and at home.

His father had by this time conceived a high opinion of him, and decided that he should enter Parliament as a young man, without adopting any other profession than politics and literature. The step seemed justified by improved family circumstances, and by the prospect of the inheritance of the Wallington estate, which the childless Sir Walter Trevelyan began about this time to hold out. In August 1863 Sir Charles wrote from Calcutta to a friend :

I have been particularly pleased at the way George has taken to Indian affairs. He has formed friendships among some of the best and ablest of the men a few years older than himself, and has imposed upon himself an improving exercise by writing about what he has seen. He will return with his mother and sister [Alice] in October. An opening will I hope soon appear for his getting into Parliament. You know how much I have it at heart. It will be much the best for him, and I do not think it will be bad for the public—to give up his whole life to public affairs.

On his return from India early in 1864 my father made his début in London society. He used afterwards to say that the ' 'sixties ' were the last decade that saw anything of ' Society ' in the old sense of the word—not a mere juxtaposition in one city of parallel sets of wealthy people, but one supreme set recognised by all others as being ' Society' *par excellence*. Entrance could neither be demanded nor purchased. The keys were held by the dames of certain great political and territorial houses, who in due consultation with their lords opened their portals to some not born within the magic circle, most often for political, sometimes for literary or personal reasons.

In the days of the Merry Monarch, the Court of Whitehall had constituted 'Society.' But ever since the Revolution, Parliament had been the heart of the aristocratic social system, and it was so still, *consule Palmerston*, when my father first came to London. To turn over the pages of the *Owl*, a politico-social magazine to which he contributed,[1] and to read his *Ladies in Parliament*, will give the modern historian, brought up in the more specialised world of our own day, a glimpse of the not ungracious connection that existed aforetime between politics, society and literature. That connection had flourished famously at Holland House, had made the world in which the Pitts and the Foxes moved, had had Gibbon and Macaulay for supporters, and still affected the Parliamentary atmosphere out of which the Reform Bill of 1867 emerged, destined to make an end of all that order of things.

Each great political hostess had, behind her London mansion, her lord's country house. Society moved out of town with the revolving season, though sadly hampered by the ever lengthening sessions of Parliament. In the country houses were sometimes found strange and wonderful folk sojourning in those tents of

[1] Its glory has long departed, but in its day it was famous enough to take a place in an advertisement that is still remembered :
    ' They come as a boon and a blessing to men—
    The Pickwick, the Owl and the Waverley pen.'

Kedar. In 1864 the Whig aristocracy had
sheltered Garibaldi from the fury of the popular
welcome, and in the following April my father
wrote from the Ashburtons' :

Carlyle, woe is me, has left. He enjoyed himself
extremely, and was delighted to find a place where he
could walk about in a wide-awake without being called
' Garibaldi ' by the small boys.

Socially a Whig, my father became a Radical
in politics. It was characteristic of him that he
learnt his new faith not from John Stuart Mill,
whom he reverenced at a distance but regarded
as a bit of a bore at close quarters, and as out of
his element in the House. It was John Bright who
touched some chord in his moral nature, always
prone to hero-worship. In 1865 Bright loomed
large, as the monstrous crow overshadowing all
that gay Society of the privileged. The American
Civil War, disregarding the path mapped out for
it by *Punch*, *The Times* and the Whig and Tory
leaders, had had the effrontery to end as Bright
had wished and foretold. The fellow was
becoming a force to be reckoned with. He was
ceasing to be an Ishmael ; he was about to
become an Institution. Meanwhile he was more
loudly abused than ever—until Gladstone took
him into partnership after Palmerston's death, and
Disraeli deftly passed his Franchise programme
into law. During these culminating passages in
the tribune's strange career, my father, as a new
member, often sat close below him in the House,
and the two exchanged remarks as they watched

together those hot Reform Bill debates. The
tried and formidable champion was touched by
the homage of the brilliant youngster from a
world in many ways so different from his own, and
for the most part still so unfriendly. What, I
wonder, did Bright think of these lines, flung in
the face of his enemies by his youthful admirer?

Since ever party strife began the world is still the same,
And Radicals from age to age are held the fairest game.
As in the troubled days of Rome each curled and scented
    jackass
Who lounged along the Sacred Way heehawed at Caius
    Gracchus,
So now all paltry jesters run their maiden wit to flesh on
A block of rugged Saxon oak, that shews no light im-
    pression ;
At which whoe'er aspires to chop had better guard his eye,
And toward the nearest cover bolt, if once the splinters
    fly.

Towards Gladstone my father felt no such
personal attraction, though full of admiring
wonder at his genius and moral power. If the
young Cambridge Liberal had got on as well with
the paragon of the Oxford movement as he did
with the Rochdale Quaker, he would have risen
higher than he did in the political world. But
as early as 1867 I note an ominous sentence in a
letter to his sister Alice :

Travelled part of the way with Gladstone. He was
reading nothing but a silly little *Church* goody book.

Any other sort of goody book would have been
more easily pardoned in a Liberal leader of those

days, for domestic politics were about to turn on the struggle for the entrenchments of Church privilege—the Universities, Church Rates, Education and the Irish Establishment. On most of these questions Gladstone did indeed most unexpectedly take the anti-Church side, but his mentality was not that of his supporters ; he arrived at the same point as they by a more circuitous route, and with much more reluctance. My father belonged to the younger generation of Oxford and Cambridge men who had little to do with the Oxford movement except to react against it. They were leagued to open the Universities to all, irrespective of religion—an idea utterly repugnant to Gladstone until the year when he put it into law. Perhaps no more important legislative change has been made in English institutions since the first Reform Bill than the abolition of the Church monopoly of Oxford and Cambridge, accomplished without the destruction of the Colleges themselves, or of anything else of value in the University tradition.

This Tests Act of 1871, which threw open Oxford and Cambridge to the nation irrespective of creed, was the outcome of a long agitation, conducted both inside and outside the two Universities, by a group of which my father, the Sidgwicks, Henry Jackson, Dicey and their friends were very prominent members. Never before or since were the younger dons of the two elder Universities drawn so closely together as when they had a common task to perform and a common battle to fight. The *Ad Eundem* dining club originated from this inter-University alliance in the cause of academic reform. The crisis began when Henry Sidgwick resigned his Trinity Fellowship, because he could no longer conscientiously say he believed in the Church formulas, of which he had been obliged to declare his acceptance. Two years later the Liberal Government passed the Tests Act which brought the required relief. In all this my father was deeply and actively concerned during his early career in Parliament, while his dearest friends were involved in it to the point of sacrificing their careers and fortunes on the altar of conscience.[1]

He had entered the House of Commons at the General Election of 1865. It was 'Palmerston's election,' when the popularity of the veteran Prime Minister won a majority which he did not live to employ and was fain to bequeath, by an irony of fate, to very different use by Russell and Gladstone. On that occasion my father was elected for Tynemouth, a small borough of an old-world character that it lost in the Reform and Redistribution two years later. Hitherto the Tories had reigned there supreme, under the patronage of the Duke of Northumberland and

[1] My father's many Oxford friendships originated in these days and in this atmosphere. In 1864 he was persuaded by his young Oxford friends to sit for an Oriel Fellowship, but his classics had grown rusty in India and proved no longer up to the highest examination level. Years afterwards he was made an Honorary Fellow of Oriel. He appreciated this honour greatly, and used to keep on his writing-table a frame containing two photographs, one of the gate of Oriel, the other of the Great Gate of his own Trinity, which had also made him an Honorary Fellow. As I am Fellow of the one College and Honorary Fellow of the other, I keep this paternal trophy in my turn.

the great shipowners. The Liberals of Tynemouth had been ' an intimidated, insignificant
party, disowned by the county people and deserted
by the leading townsmen of their party.' So
wrote my father in the autumn of 1864, but his
arrival as candidate, with strong outside backing
and a power of oratory, had put a new spirit into
the place. A great shipowner joined his committee
and drove him round on the box of a four-in-hand.
It came to be understood that the election would
turn on the possession of the Chirton estate on the
edge of the borough, containing farmers and other
tenants who always voted with their landlord
whoever he might be. Sir Walter Trevelyan of
Wallington in the same county of Northumberland,
who already regarded my father as his future heir,
aided him to buy the Chirton estate for £61,000.
It was sold again after the election, having served
its purpose. In July 1865, as the victor of
Tynemouth, my father went down to Lancashire
to aid Gladstone in the electoral battle he was
fighting there, ' unmuzzled ' by his rejection for
Oxford University. Gladstone told him that
Tynemouth was ' the most surprising victory of
the election. He was very excited and gushing,
and Mrs. Gladstone was wild with interest and
eagerness.'

The fact that my father, of all people, first
entered Parliament by such a road as the Chirton
estate, indicates how little of a Radical he then
was, and what were the limits of the electoral
reform that had been effected in 1832.

If the Election of 1865 was Palmerston's, the Election of 1868 was Gladstone's. It was held under the new working-class franchise for the boroughs, passed the year before. My father too had changed in the interval. Three years of sitting under Bright in the House, and watching real politics close at hand, had made him a more responsible and serious man, and something of a political purist. For the new Parliament he found a constituency of the new kind, the Scottish Border Burghs, that suited him better than Tynemouth. His Scottish radical friends sent him up to every Parliament from 1868 until the Home Rule Election of 1886. It was indeed a happy connection for all concerned. Hawick, Selkirk and Galashiels were rich in the historic lore in which he delighted. They were the land of Sir Walter Scott, though not of 'the shirra's' politics. And they lay scarce forty miles from Wallington in Northumberland, where my father was now always welcome as the favourite guest of Sir Walter Trevelyan and his wife Pauline.

That talented lady was the wise Egeria of Swinburne, Ruskin and the Pre-raphaelites—ardent spirits who consorted much at Wallington, regarding my father tolerantly as an intelligent Philistine who had the run of the house, but who was careful and troubled about matters with which they had no concern. Yet in his own way my father also was an artist. In 1866, at the height of the struggle over the Reform Bill, he had published his *Ladies in Parliament*, the most mature effort of his talent for light verse. It was his last as well as his most successful performance in that sort. In later life no one was less addicted to rhyme. The power, he said, totally went from him before he was thirty. Thenceforward he was historian and statesman—nothing more.

The *Ladies in Parliament*, for all its merits, is to-day more completely forgotten than the *Horace at Athens*, because whereas Cambridge still exists, the London society and politics of 1866 have disappeared utterly into the deep of time. But the opening of the Aristophanic chorus in praise of the sturdy conservatism of our ancestors may still be quoted as the last effort of his youthful muse :

We much revere our sires, who were a mighty race of
    men.
For every glass of port we drink they nothing thought of
    ten.
They dwelt above the foulest drains. They breathed the
    closest air.
They had their yearly twinge of gout, and little seemed
    to care.
They set those meddling people down for Jacobins or
    fools
Who talked of public libraries, and grants to normal
    schools ;
Since common folks who read, and write, and like their
    betters speak,
Want something more than pipes, and beer, and sermons
    once a week.
And therefore both by land and sea their match they
    rarely met,
But made the name of Britain great, and ran her deep
    in debt.

They seldom stopped to count the foe, nor sum the
    moneys spent,
But clenched their teeth and straight ahead with sword
    and musket went.
And, though they thought if trade were free that England
    ne'er would thrive,
They freely gave their blood for Moore and Wellington
    and Clive.
And, though they burned their coal at home, nor fetched
    their ice from Wenham,
They played the man before Quebec and stormed the
    lines at Blenheim.
When sailors lived on mouldy bread, and lumps of rusty
    pork,
No Frenchman dared his face to show between the
    Downs and Cork.
But now that Jack gets beef and greens, and next his
    skin wears flannel,
The *Standard* says we've not a ship in plight to keep the
    Channel.

I shall always deeply regret that my father did
not write reminiscences of his early life, and of
that brilliant, long-vanished society in which as a
young man he was so full a participant. Once
only, in his extreme old age, he was moved to
send some 'Recollections of Disraeli' to the
Saturday Review.

My first introduction to Mr. Disraeli was not
auspicious. I was chosen by the Borough of Tynemouth at the General Election of July, 1865. A great
number of new members, and young members, were
returned ; we each of us knew many of the others ; and,
during the ensuing autumn, and early winter—what
with foreign travel, field-sports, and country-house
parties—we fleeted the time merrily and carelessly, as

people then did in that golden world. The custom had not yet begun of indicating the position of guests at the dinner-table by cards inscribed with their names ; and a person with quick eyes, who knew his own mind, found his account in this omission. Holding no office, and possessing no social precedence, I always went into the dining-room among the very last, and often without a lady ; and therefore, by deciding rapidly, and acting promptly, I generally succeeded in planting myself with the company which was most to my liking. But the advantages of the system were counter-balanced by one serious, and by no means imaginary, danger. If there was a very formidable personage present, the chair next to him was apt to be the only seat left vacant for the last person who entered the dining-room.

Towards the end of the year 1865, the Dowager Lady Cowper invited a large number of guests to her seat at Wrest, in Bedfordshire. On the first evening Mr. Disraeli took down the hostess ; and, to my dismay, there was no chair for me to occupy except that which stood empty on his other side. It was a more trying ordeal even than I anticipated ; for Mr. Disraeli did not speak to me once all through the dinner, or after the ladies left. At last a sort of general conversation arose across the table, about the difficulties and distresses of scientific inventors, whose fields of discovery were poached upon by intruders ; and then I broke silence, and timidly and respectfully asked Mr. Disraeli whether he had a strong opinion on the Patent Laws. ' I have,' he replied, ' no strong opinion upon any subject in the world ' ; and that was the only remark which he addressed to me from the first moment to the last. It was a relief when we adjourned to the drawing-room, where I found refuge among people who were glad to talk, and quite willing to be talked to.

Next morning the home-covers were beaten for

pheasants, including beds of shrubs on the lawns immediately round the house. I seem to remember a
woodcock being killed, or missed, in dangerous proximity
to a statue of William the Third ; a monarch who in his
life-time had no special objection to the smell of powder,
or the whistling of lead. The men of the party, in their
shooting-clothes and gaiters, assembled in a small room
on the other side of the hall from the dining-room,
where breakfast was laid. I was standing in front of
the fire when the door opened, and Mr. Disraeli entered,
clad in velvet of a showy and cheerful colour. He
walked straight up to me, and said that on the previous
evening he had not been aware that I was the son of
his old and valued friend Sir Charles Trevelyan ; and
then he started off into a very lively anecdote—told
in old-fashioned and almost obsolete, but exquisitely
comical terms—at the expense of the then Duke of
Argyll, whom he did not profess to regard with any
great affection or reverence.

From that time forwards, for many months to come,
he treated me with a flattering and rather mocking
freedom, quite irresistible to younger men whom he was
desirous to conciliate. His indulgent irony was inter-
spersed with archaic phrases which he was fond of
employing, and which gave a flavour to his conversation.
I saw something of him and of Mrs. Disraeli, in his own
house, and the sincerity of his good-will was confirmed
by things which I was told by colleagues of his who sat
with him on the front Opposition bench in the House
of Commons. I made my maiden speech, which was
far from being a success,[1] when seconding a Resolution
in favour of University Reform. Some Conservative

---

[1] In the matter of maiden speeches, my father long afterwards wrote on
the margin of his copy of Galsworthy's *Silver Spoon* (chap. v), ' I remember
some one telling me his feeling after he had got some way with his maiden
speech. He felt as if the Speaker would rise and say : " Well, we can
stand a good deal in this House, but this is too much. The Honourable
gentleman must resume his seat." I think the man who said this to me
was Davenport Bromley.'

ex-ministers were comparing my performance un-
favourably with that of the mover of the Resolution,
who was a practised and mature speaker of high forensic
fame. 'That may be,' said Mr. Disraeli, 'but all the
same I bet on the black-un'; and at that age I was
black indeed. On another occasion a family friend of
ours—a governor of the Bank of England, a man of
social importance, and a general favourite—pointed me
out to Mr. Disraeli in the House, and said that he used
to tip Sir Charles Trevelyan when a boy at the Charterhouse. 'Oh,' said Mr. Disraeli, 'so you *pouched* his
father. Why don't you *pouch* him too? He would be
pretty sure to like it.'

When in the General Election of 1865 my father,
as the victor of Tynemouth, had gone down to
Lancashire to the aid of the Liberal battle there,
the Gladstones had not been the only people with
whom he had associated. He then for the first
time in his life came across the Philipses of
Manchester, and laid the foundation of something better than his political fortunes. Robert
Needham Philips, my maternal grandfather, whom
I well recollect, was a merchant and politician of
the old school, a strenuous supporter of Free Trade
and Reform, a Unitarian but not a precisian,
giving the impression of a hearty squire of the old
world rather than of a follower of Cobden as he
actually was. He was a born electioneer, and
my father's first sight of him was as he sat in his
shirt sleeves at the table in Gladstone's Committee
Rooms, ordering the Lancashire politicians about
like a captain on the quarter-deck in action. He
was at once captivated by my father's youthful

gifts and by his prowess as an orator. From the first he smiled on the prospect of having him for a son-in-law, and it early became apparent that a mutual attachment had arisen between his daughter Caroline and the young member for Tynemouth. They were speedily engaged, but obstacles no less speedily arose. Robert Philips, important as he was in Lancashire trade and politics, was not then independent. His elder brother Mark Philips, one of the first two members elected for Manchester after its enfranchisement in 1832, still held his younger brother in leading strings as regards this world's goods and prospects. Mark was a strong and in many respects an admirable man, but he had not generous and enlightened feelings on all subjects. Himself a bachelor, he looked to see his niece Caroline allied to a lord. He caused her father to dismiss her *fiancé* with scant courtesy. My mother would certainly never have married anyone else, whether peer or commoner. Her firm and silent gentleness was sorely tried for two years, but not by any weakening on my father's part.

It was in these circumstances, immediately after his dismissal by the Philips brothers, that his Garibaldian adventure took place, of which fortunately he has left a record, published in *The Times* of 1924, in the form of a letter to Lady Desborough, whose father was Julian Henry Fane, son of the eleventh Earl of Westmorland. The allusion in the first sentence of my father's letter is to the circumstance that Lady Desborough had read his ' Cawnpore ' to her two noble sons who lost their lives in the Great War.

Wallington, Cambo, Morpeth,
June 24, 1924.

Dear Lady Desborough,

I was deeply grateful, deeply interested, on receiving your letter, and even more moved and touched than interested by knowing who they were to whom in old days you had read my ' Cawnpore.' I will at once avail myself of your permission to tell you my one, and only, interview with your father.

It took place in the last week of October, 1867. The great French Exhibition was in progress at Paris. All the rulers of the world were fraternizing, or pretending to fraternize, there as the guests of Louis Napoleon ; and Europe was everywhere in profound peace except in a single spot ; for Garibaldi had invaded the Roman territory with about 10,000 men—the largest, though very far from the best, army that he ever led. The Italian Government disowned him, and (publicly at all events) disapproved his action. The French Army of Occupation, which had been withdrawn from Rome, was being hurried back again to help, and save, the Pope ; and the news of a great battle at, or near, Rome was daily expected.

I had gone over to Paris to spend a week, and see the Exhibition. I was then a very young member of Parliament, at the end of my second session. One morning, towards the close of my intended stay in Paris, a letter arrived by post containing most unexpected, and very serious, personal news. I was greatly overset, and in the circumstances, as they presented themselves to me, my one and only feeling was a craving for change of scene and thought, and an irresistible impulse towards enterprise and action. I was impatient to start at once for Italy ; and my sincere opinions on the Italian question seemed to justify my going there. But I could not hope to cross the Alps without a passport ; I had very little ready money left ; and I disliked the idea of spending another night in Paris. So I went to the British Embassy, and sent in my name. Your father, who then was Secretary to the Embassy, desired me to be shown into his room. We had never met ; we did not know each other by sight ; but the universal opinion of London society about him, and more especially the affection with which his intimate friend William Harcourt (who was excessively kind to me) regarded and spoke of him, aroused in me a strong desire to see him, and inspired an instant confidence in him. I am convinced that he detected that I was under the influence of strong emotion, from some unexplained cause ; and his kindness was instantly aroused, and certainly proved itself most efficient. He at once, as if it was the most natural thing in the world, gave me the passport, and told me that I need not mind knowing no Italian, for I need only say *Sono Deputato Inglese,* and every one would help me forward on my journey. I asked him to give me a letter of identification in order to borrow money from a bank, but he said that I should have all I could do to get ready to start by the Night Express ; and then and there, without ever having seen my face before, he handed over to me thirty pounds of his own, in French money. I never saw him again ; I have loved him ever since ; and I am glad to know that he was one of those whom the world did not misjudge, but appreciated at his true value.

The next few days passed as in a dream. I went by the night express, over Mont Cenis in the diligence ; and through Turin, and thence to Florence—which at that time was the capital of Italy. Everywhere the three Italian words which he had given me were a talisman which carried me forward rapidly, and with the evident good will, and unexpressed good wishes, of all who heard them. The first person whom I met at the Hotel Europa at the end of the Ponte Vecchio was

G

Lord Lorne, who then, as I always thought him afterwards, was as handsome and friendly a young fellow as I ever knew. He had come down straight to Florence, from Vienna, on the same errand as myself; but our Ambassador in Italy, Sir Augustus Paget, had told him that the French troops had landed ; that the Italian Government deeply disapproved of Garibaldi's action ; that the business was hopeless ; and that he had much better desist from his intention. However, when Lorne found that I was bent on going on, he said that he would go with me. We travelled South as far as Foligno, which was more than halfway to Rome ; but there all railway communication ceased, and no trains were allowed to run. But when the Stationmaster learned who we were he told us to come down to the station next morning, and he would send us forward, on an engine, across the frontier, and into Garibaldi's camp. Next morning early we went down to the station and learned that on the previous day Garibaldi had been entirely defeated in a decisive battle at Mentana, and that he was returning in a train with his Staff and his personal followers, and might be expected within a couple of hours. At about 10 or 11 in the morning the train came in, and stayed some while at the station. We presented ourselves respectfully to the General, and he received us simply and cordially—Lorne as the son of those who had been his principal entertainers during his visit to England in 1864, and me as the Member for Tynemouth and North Shields, to which port he had sailed as a merchant-captain in the intervals of his soldiering, and where he had friends, about whose welfare he inquired.

It was the worst moment in his long life of uphill struggle ; but he met, and surpassed, my expectation of him as a noble and modest hero ; something more homely than I expected, but none the less lovable and admirable on that account. Outside the carriage I talked with Ricciotti Garibaldi, his younger son, a bright, handsome fellow of 18 or 20, in his red shirt and grey flannel trousers. Ricciotti told me that the fighting on the previous day at Mentana had been very severe. The Italians more than held their own against the Papal troops until the French came in, armed with the breech-loader Chassepot, a new weapon in Italy, of which ' the sound was continuous, like *tonnerre*,' he said. So I suppose that we talked in French.

Garibaldi asked us very kindly to travel with him in his carriage to Florence ; but we were unwilling to intrude on him at such a time, and got into a compartment with some of his people. The train travelled slowly, stopping at all the larger towns ; and everywhere enormous masses of people were awaiting him. No one spoke a word ; no one attempted a cheer. While the train was there they gathered on each side of his carriage like a great swarm of bees, to be as near him as they could and to have a chance of seeing his countenance. The November night set in before we reached Filigne, a small town about 25 miles south of Florence. There we found the platform of the station occupied by a full company of the famous Bersaglieri, and a contingent of gendarmes. They turned the whole party of us out of the train and informed Garibaldi that he must consider himself under arrest, which he refused to do.

For about an hour the crowded scene was quiet enough. They brought out a straw kitchen chair for Garibaldi, who tilted it back against the wall of the building, and sat with his feet hanging negligently down. From time to time there was parleying, but nothing came of it. At length all of a sudden the Italian officers gave a sharp word of command, and the soldiers stood to attention and prepared their arms as if to fire. Some of the bystanders disappeared round a corner, starting to run quicker than I ever saw people start before in my life ; but the red-shirted Garibaldians drew their pistols, and gathered up in close order in front of the General. Lorne and I were standing on the step of the railway carriage between the two parties ; but we felt nothing except the most intense interest, as if we were watching a historical drama out of a private stage box.

At this moment a young man with curling black hair came out from among the Garibaldians, and, standing beneath a lighted gas-jet, addressed the soldiers in two or three stirring sentences, which even I made shift to understand, telling them that they were fighting ' against heroes, against Italy.' I heard him speak once again, perhaps 30 years afterwards, when his still curling hair was white, as Prime Minister in the Italian Parliament ; for it was Crispi. Garibaldi, however, thought it was time to end the business, and intimated that he should make no resistance if they chose to arrest him by force. So two gendarmes took him by the shoulders and two by the knees, and carried him past us within a yard of where we were standing. Often and often, during our many visits to Rome, I thought of that scene when I looked at his noble equestrian statue dominating the city and the Vatican, from the summit of the Janiculan Hill, where no effigy of Imperator, or Kaiser, or Pope had ever been allowed to be erected.

They added three or four carriages to the train, filled it up with soldiers, put the General and his sons into their compartment, and turned the rest of us out on to the platform, and bade us shift for ourselves. This did not suit our views ; so, when the train began to move, Lorne and I jumped into a carriage full of Bersaglieri, who smiled at us benevolently from under their broad hats. No doubt they took us for a couple of young swells who found ourselves in a scrape, and wished to get out of it on the cheapest terms ; and so perhaps we were. The train stopped outside the walls of Florence and we forthwith alighted, and made our way across fields into the city. If I recollect aright Lorne went to our Embassy to inform Sir Augustus Paget of what had happened. I do not think that on that occasion I went with him.

Those are the sights and experiences, and those are the well-timed and invaluable good offices, which I owe to your father.   And so, dear Lady Desborough, I hope you will forgive the length of my story for the sake of the gratitude which I felt, and shall always feel, towards him.

I remain yours very sincerely,

GEORGE OTTO TREVELYAN.

And so he returned to Florence to brood over his forbidden attachment. There he found a friend in need.   Sixty years later he wrote :

Lady Frederick Cavendish, her husband and myself spent every evening together at Florence.   She said she knew there was something the matter with me, and challenged me to tell her what it was.   I told her, and she kept the secret, which I cannot remember telling anyone else.   And she gave me an eager and beautiful sympathy.

Two years followed during which my father and my mother, thus forcibly separated, were not happy.   But my father could distract himself with exciting and successful political work, the active throb of the great world, and a host of friends. Long afterwards he wrote to my wife an episode of this period :

It will be delightful talking over Auvergne with you when we meet.   I went there in the Whitsuntide preceding the July when we made up our marriage in 1869 ; and I was not very happy ; but I had two great friends with me, Belper and Cobham.   And I principally remember the personal incidents.   Once, waiting at a road-side station, we were talking of throwing the cricket-ball, whether anyone went much over 110 yards.   Cobham said he had thrown 120, and had thrown a stone 150 yards.

I stepped, then and there, 150 paces ; and he just stuck his umbrella in the ground, and threw a stone over my head.

At length, in July 1869, the formidable Mark Philips suddenly surrendered.   That day my father wrote to my mother :

And so it is all over ; and we are to be happy and sorry, and overworked and idle, and successful and unlucky together all the rest of our lives.   Your father was very, very kind about it ; and it is pleasant to see how relieved and happy he seems.

A few days later ' Uncle Mark ' wrote to my father :

The days of Clarissa Harlowe are fortunately known no more, and Carry declares that she can expect happiness only as your wife.   I fear you will not felicitate yourself upon becoming connected with a gouty old uncle, but I will try to behave well and not be cross.

That same evening he received another letter from a different quarter :

Dear Mr. Trevelyan,
    Didn't I always so say !   And ain't I the very wisest and best of prophets and advisers ?   God grant you may both be happy as we are, for many long years.   Very sincerely yours,
                                    LUCY C. F. CAVENDISH.

Sunt lacrymae rerum.
    A few days later my father recounted, in a letter to Henry Sidgwick, ' Uncle Mark's ' surrender, which he described as ' most unexpected,' adding ' On the whole it is much better than if it had gone smoothly two years back.'

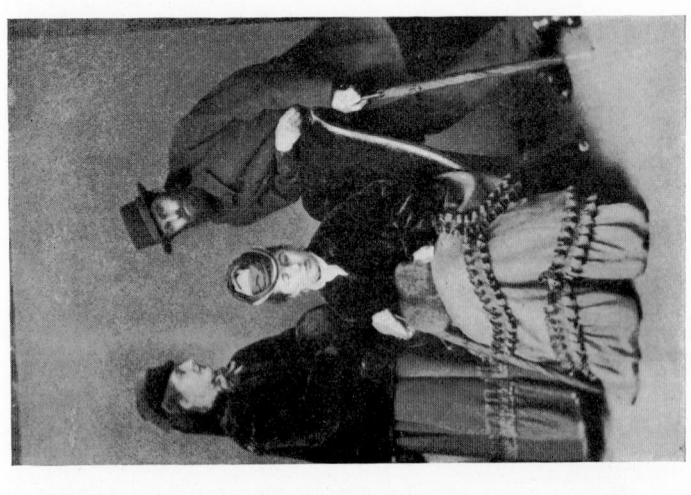

G. O. Trevelyan and his Wife Caroline   About 1870.
His Sister Alice seated.

G. O. Trevelyan and his Sister Alice
About 1865.

In September 1869 they were married, the happiest event of two long and happy lives.

In this business my mother had shown quiet and effective powers of resistance. But she had not the active force of character that imposes its will on others. In years to come her husband and her three sons all represented the active principle working in various directions, and she the passive. But the beauty of a quiet character and of a wisdom that seldom speaks and never loudly, was deeply felt by all who knew her. Her fullest self-expression was in the admirable landscapes which she painted wherever she went—at home, in Switzerland or in Italy. Her reading in modern literature was almost as wide as my father's, though he had the field of the classics to himself. How many hours in the course of sixty years he spent in reading to her aloud ! It seemed as if all that was best in English prose and poetry had been composed for their joint delight. They were very seldom apart. During one of these brief separations, in 1908, he wrote to my wife, ' I never am unhappy for a few days with work and solitude ; for that amount of solitude, brief, and at long intervals, introduces an element of contemplation and recognition into one's feeling about the person whose presence makes one's life.' They grew into one another by mind and habit so that I used often to wonder how one could survive alone. And that impossible experiment fortunately only lasted from her death in January to his in August 1928.

CHAPTER IV

POLITICS, LITERATURE AND FAMILY LIFE, 1870–
1885. IN AND OUT OF OFFICE. *Macaulay.*
Fox. IRELAND

THE General Election of 1868, held under the
new working-class franchise in the boroughs, gave
Gladstone power to form the first and greatest of
his Ministries. Although, for reasons to be stated,
my father was not long in office, he saw realised
during the six years of that government most of
the reforms which he and his friends had at heart.
He himself had been the chief advocate of one of
these measures, the Abolition of Purchase in the
Army. The existing system barred promotion to
officers of small private means, and rendered the
prizes of the profession the monopoly of the well-
to-do. Sir Charles Trevelyan had long been the
enemy of the Purchase system, and after his son
entered the House supplied him with powder and
shot for the campaign. 'Public opinion,' writes
Morley in his 'Life of Gladstone,' 'had been
mainly roused by Mr. Trevelyan, who now first
made his mark in that assembly where he was
destined to do admirable work and achieve high
eminence and popularity.'

In 1871 the question came to its crisis. The
Franco-Prussian War made Englishmen for a few
months interested in the state of their army, so
easily forgotten at other times. The opportunity
was seized, and the victory was won by the brilliant
tactics of Gladstone, who overrode the legislative
resistance of the House of Lords by obtaining a
Royal Warrant to abolish Purchase. The Queen
' made no sort of objection to signing the warrant '
after receiving a formal, signed minute of the
Cabinet requesting her to do so with reasons given.
But conservative feeling on the subject ran very
hot in fashionable society and among the army
chiefs with the Duke of Cambridge at their head.
The old system died biting hard, and my father's
championship of the victorious cause did him no
good in some quarters.

Another project, also sprung from my grandfather's fertile brain, was the opening of the Civil
Service to entry by competitive examination.
This change had been coming in bit by bit for a
dozen years past, very slowly during the last years
of Palmerston, who had thought it great nonsense.
At length in 1870 Gladstone made its application
general. Competition stopped aristocratic and
political jobbing and replaced the Lord Dundreary
type of civil servant by the more active and
intelligent product of the Universities. But the
old system of patronage appointments found in
the ranks of the Civil Service itself an advocate
whose opinions on any subject will be of interest
to posterity. Anthony Trollope in his ' Auto-

biography' tells us that his novel 'The Three Clerks'

is chiefly noticeable to me from the fact that in it I introduced a character under the name of Sir Gregory Hardlines, by which I intended to lean very heavily on that loathed scheme of competitive examination, of which at that time Sir Charles Trevelyan was the great apostle. Sir Gregory Hardlines was intended for Sir Charles Trevelyan—as anyone at the time would know who had taken an interest in the Civil Service. ' We always call him Sir Gregory,' Lady Trevelyan said to me afterwards, when I came to know her and her husband. I never learned to love competitive examination ; but I became, and am, very fond of Sir Charles Trevelyan.

Church privilege also underwent its full share of retrenchment, in the Disestablishment of the Irish Church in 1869, and two years later by the opening of Oxford and Cambridge to all creeds by the Tests Act, which has already been mentioned. But Forster's Education Act of 1870, one of the most important measures of this great Ministry, was a bitter disappointment to half the Liberal Party and to all the Nonconformists, because, while establishing publicly managed ' Board Schools,' it increased the State Grant to Church Schools, with a view to rendering them a permanent part of the new educational system. Into that controversy, which in changed forms is with us still, God forbid that I should here enter. I will be content to print the letter in which my father explained to his constituents the reasons why he resigned office on the question.

June 29, 1870.

Dear Mr. Wilson,

I have resigned office because I am unable to support the increase of the grant to denominational schools, which is a main condition and integral part of the Government policy. A private member is at liberty to support the Bill, and to oppose the grant : but a member of the Government can make no distinction between the different portions of the scheme. I regard this matter as one not of expediency, but of right and wrong : just as a conservative would regard a proposal to curtail the powers and resources of the Established Church. The election which preceded the abolition of the Irish Church was welcomed by a large section of the liberal party as an opportunity of protesting against the public endowment and recognition of creeds. It is not every day that the people in general get hold of a broad, simple, and true idea as an article of political faith : and to inspire such an idea is the only method of extending political education through the mass of a community. Nothing has tended so much to elevate and ennoble public opinion as the conviction of multitudes of electors that in voting for religious equality in Ireland they were establishing a rule of policy which would influence the decision of all religious and educational questions throughout the entire kingdom. On the other hand I do not know anything which will more profoundly demoralise public opinion than the discovery that a principle, in which men have learned to believe, and for which they have made great sacrifices, is supposed to have only a partial application ; and that, after dealing a death blow to the endowment of denominations in Ireland, we are to spend additional hundreds of thousands a year on denominations in England. Nothing but the belief that a vital principle is at stake would justify me in leaving a Government which has made good so many claims upon the respect of the country.

I remain,

Yours truly,

G. O. TREVELYAN.

His Scottish Radical constituents were convinced by this reasoning as easily as the Nonconformists of England. But many politicians thought my father's action quixotic ; the view expressed by the *Spectator* was, I expect, very commonly held.

Mr. G. O. Trevelyan, Civil Lord of the Admiralty, appears to be possessed of that extremely rare and inconvenient article, an over-sensitive conscience. He cannot endure to vote for a Bill increasing the grant to denominational schools, and has consequently resigned. When an ambitious man gives up his chance of a career from a conscientious scruple we have nothing to do but to respect his principles, even if we cannot, as in this case, appreciate his action.

Gladstone did not soon or easily forgive him ; he left him out of his next Government when he formed it in 1880. My father had put himself back ten years and more in the race up the ladder of political promotion, on the lower rungs of which he had made so early and so promising a start. But he never regretted his action in the retrospect.

Fortunately work and happiness were within his reach, outside the doors of office. His new family life was completely happy, and the glimpses of it

given in his letters to his sister Alice Dugdale make
pleasant reading.

Mürren,
Sept. 5, 1873.

These mountain hotels are certainly a wonderful
invention of the present generation, and a curious
illustration of its tastes. You would enjoy this place so
with your love of walking. Among other things one gets
rid of the worse sort of tourists. People must have something good about them who come up here. Carry suffers
acutely from her first separation from the little boys, but
consoled herself by buying Charley some little wooden
Swiss animals.[1]

A few days later he writes to Alice from Milan :

We are reading Gibbon. The excellence of it is
astonishing. That a man should have read through such
an amorphous immeasurable mass of antique rubbish and
yet retain such wit, vigour and imagination . . .

The force of this panegyric will be admitted
with a sigh by anyone who has ever attempted
to write ' serious history ' from documents. Again
he writes to his sister :

We are reading Hogg's life of Shelley. It is an extra-
ordinarily amusing book. For the first time since reading
Monte Christo at Harrow I find myself counting the pages
that remain. It is a wonderfully amusing compound of
vanity, silliness and cleverness, and gives a better picture
of Shelley than any book gives of any other individual.

He found something nearer to a model for his
own line of biography in Carlyle's ' Sterling,'
which he read again and again. Well as he knew

---

[1] My brother Charles Philips (now Sir Charles) was born in 1870 and
my brother Robert Calverley, the poet, in 1872.

Carlyle personally, he never could understand how the master failed—or thought he failed—to get happiness from the act of writing such entrancing history books. It always remained a mystery to him how Carlyle could give intellectual pleasure so abundantly to others, yet himself groan daily over the task. For his part, the biographer of Macaulay belonged to his uncle's more eupeptic school of reading and writing.

In these years and in these ways he was preparing himself for the most important undertaking of his life. A wise instinct forbade him to begin the ' Life of Macaulay ' until his powers were at their full and his experience of life and letters as complete as it ever became. The documents had been long at his disposal, but he only began work upon them in earnest after Liberal members had been endowed with the relative leisure of opposition by Disraeli's triumph at the General Election of February 1874. Till then he had been too loyal a supporter of the Government, from which he had resigned, to absent himself from debates and divisions in the interest of literature. A man of nervous artistic temperament, he could not drive two great tasks abreast. He needed to be wholly absorbed either in speech-making or in authorship, and it drove him frantic to be fiddling with both at once. The ' Macaulay ' and the ' Fox ' were the fruits of six years of opposition ; the ' American Revolution ' of final retirement from politics.

It cannot be doubted that he was wise to post-

LADY TREVELYAN
(Hannah More Macaulay)
About 1870.

pone work on his uncle's biography as long as he did, yet his delay was a grief to his mother, who desired to see her brother's life told while she was there to read it, and feared that her son was dallying too long. She died in 1873, carrying great memories to the grave, and leaving her husband and children to feel that the strong pillar of their house had fallen.

Two years of intense but joyous work, only broken at the end by a very severe illness, enabled my father to produce the 'Life of Macaulay,' which came out in the first days of March 1876. A fortnight earlier, I had arrived in the world. The happy and the troublesome activities that follow close on the birth of a baby or of a book synchronised in the following weeks, and I had the reflex honour of being christened George Macaulay.

The book has been very generally regarded as the model of that particular type of biography. It was certainly the type best calculated to do justice to Macaulay. His conversation, good as it was, would not have been worthy of the method that Boswell applied to Johnson, and Hogg to Shelley. Public interest in him would have been buried under the seven volumes with which Lockhart could venture to load the stupendous popularity of Scott. He was not sufficiently odd or subtle to give flavour to a thin volume in the biographical taste of the present day, half psychology and half journalism. His greatest strength had always lain in his pen, and my father's copious but wisely selected quotations from his letters and journals, strung together by a political and personal narrative in the biographer's own most brilliant style, has added something permanent to our literature.[1]

There lies before me as I write a stack of reviews and letters of congratulation to my father on his book, from men still remembered and from men long forgotten. To handle such papers after fifty years is to pick up a wreath, once so blooming, full of delicious odour to the recipient, but dusty and long withered now. One of them alone still seems instinct with life, the tribute of Carlyle to the record of his great co-rival, whom living he had not cared to understand, and by whom he had not been understood. Certainly it was the certificate my father most valued in this world. He has printed it at the beginning of the later editions of the book which it praised with such generosity.

> 5 Cheyne Row, Chelsea,
> 3 April 1876.

Dear Trevelyan,

Yesterday I finished the ' Life of Lord Macaulay,' which you were so kind and mindful as to send me on the Monday morning previous, and which has given me a week's reading, by far the best I have had for a long while. I thank you much for that act of beneficence ; and cannot forbear, at the same time, testifying that I think it a work excellently done, and that will through long times be interesting to many readers. I have nowhere found in

---

[1] Eleven volumes of Macaulay's journal now lie in the library of Trinity College, Cambridge. They were written for his own delectation, not for publication. My father's extracts from them were excellently made.

any biography, not even in ' Boswell's Johnson,' a human life and character more clearly, credibly and completely brought home to the conception of every intelligent reader ; nor have I, it is to be added, in all my reading found any human character that is to my notion more singular and unique. Very strange to me indeed that unexampled power of memory, of voracious reading and of clear articulate utterance ; making your Uncle a miracle to his own generation and memorable, were it only as a bit of psychology, to many generations that are coming. A man of thorough honesty, withal, and of sound human sense in regard to all practical matters, and of a most affectionate, tender and equitable nature, and such a placid and complete satisfaction with his lot, outward and inward, in this world as fills me with a cheerful amazement.

Your own part of the affair I think you have performed to admiration : nothing hidden and yet no offence given ; an excellent brief History of the period, as well as of its speaking man. In short, I can with perfect truth con-gratulate you, and say, as I believe the whole world will do, *Euge, euge !*

With many thanks,

Yours ever truly,

T. CARLYLE.

That letter of Carlyle's [he wrote to his sister] is, indeed, precious. Nothing has given me so much satisfaction as to find that the *eminent* literary men, who were not overfond of my uncle *qua* literary man, have been quite won over by his private personality. Witness Carlyle, Morley, Leslie Stephen, and Froude.

Indeed this was so far the case that John Morley went to the length of saying that the ' Life of Macaulay ' was a better book than the History of

H

England, a piece of friendly cajolery which was not likely to go very far with my father.

The appearance of the Life was a pleasant business all that spring, but it was followed in the winter by something desperately unpleasant— the Eastern Question. Disraeli aligned England with the Turkish rule over Bulgaria and Macedonia, and threatened to make her fight on its behalf. It is easy to be philosophical about it now, and to think Gladstone was too hot. But if he had not been hot we might not merely have ' put our money on the wrong horse ' as we actually did for a few years—we might have gone irretrievably to war on behalf of that decrepit and abominable animal. Gladstone may have been too much excited, but he was fundamentally right when he saw the true barrier to Russian advance not in the Turkish rule, already overripe to rottenness, but in the young national instincts of the Christian peoples of the Balkans—' the breasts of freemen ' as he styled it in the language of his oratory. Subsequent events have shown that in this matter he was more realist than Disraeli. The idealist is not on all occasions the furthest from hard fact. Disraeli understood many things that Gladstone did not understand, but Gladstone understood the power latent in nationality and Disraeli did not.

The Liberal party found itself in this great crisis feebly led by the residuary chiefs whom Gladstone had left to it on his premature retirement in 1874. Gladstone, on the wings of his passion, flew back into politics, addressing mass meetings, speaking from train windows, with the methods of a modern demagogue, but a demagogue who had in him something of the demi-god. My father, utterly on his side, ranged himself in the battle to avert war on behalf of the Turk. On December 6, 1876, he wrote to his sister Alice :

I am to speak at the Conference on Friday, which has within the last ten days assumed almost colossal proportions. I believe it to be the most imposing demonstration ever made in this country. The crisis is immense, and the responsibility involved very great. The Liberal party have joined almost to a man, except ex-Cabinet Ministers who purposely keep aloof. I feel, as one ought to try to feel on such occasions, that the *popularity* of the step is a secondary consideration. The Prime Minister has declared publicly that we are to fight for the independence of Turkey. We declare on the other hand that, as far as we are concerned, we will not fight. The future will show whether he or we will carry the country. But as to our duty, I am as clear as ever I was in my life.

So that fever of the body politic began to rage in England, and burnt on for eighteen angry months, until Disraeli returned from Berlin bringing ' peace with honour '—the honour of having put back the Macedonian Christians under the Turkish yoke and encouraged Austria to enter the Balkans. But war had been avoided and Bulgaria, in spite of Disraeli, was free.

All through the 'seventies my father was the champion of the cause of County Franchise. The agricultural labourer and the other working-

class residents in county constituencies—coal-
miners for example—had not been enfranchised
in 1867 when the vote was given to the working
class in the Parliamentary Boroughs. There were
two Englands, a democratic England of the cities,
and an aristocratic England of the shires governed
paternally by the J.P.'s and great landowners, the
countryside portrayed by Trollope. Year after
year in the 'seventies my father introduced a
Bill to assimilate the County to the Borough
Franchise. The Reform Bill of 1884–5 eventually
gave effect to this change, which he had been the
first to bring forward and had so long kept before
the eye of Parliament.

In March 1877 his name came up for ballot at
the Athenæum Club. Some of the older military
members had not even yet forgiven the enemy of
their beloved Purchase system, dead six years
before. It was understood that they were combining to blackball him. ' I am gratified,' he
wrote to Henry Sidgwick, ' by the general indignation, especially among Conservatives ; but one
foe is in this case equal to ten friends.' A strong
movement in his favour arose in the Club that was
then, even more than now, the focus of the
intellectual life of the nation. His nomination
card was signed by an unexampled galaxy of
names famous in letters, science and public life—
the photograph that was taken of it is a reminder
of the wealth of Victorian England in such names.
Carlyle, aged eighty-two, not only signed but
came down to vote and urge others to vote for

him. Next day (March 20, 1877) my father
wrote :

Dear Mr. Carlyle,

I most heartily thank you for the very signal kindness
and honour which you did me by coming to the Athenæum
Club last night. The result of the voting was : *For* 389,
against 20 ; so that I was elected by a large majority, but
at the same time under circumstances which proved that
precautions were not superfluous. The fact of your
having been present on the occasion will always be
remembered by me and mine with pride and gratitude.

In these years he often went for walks and rides
with the sage of Chelsea, over Hampstead Heath
and in the still attainable outskirts of London.
The views of the young man and the old were by
no means the same with regard to the modern
world and its chance of prospering by the help of
machinery and ballot boxes, but on history and
literature they had a mental vision not wholly dissimilar. Carlyle used to call him, with affectionate
humour, a *pullus Jovis*, a fortunate youth. On
one of their long walks, Carlyle for two hours paid
out, as he strode along, the life-story of the elder
Pitt, being desirous that his young friend should
choose that subject for his next biography, rather
than Fox, for whom the Sage cared little. His
hearer, who had heard many good talks, used ever
afterwards to say that it was the best talk he ever
heard from the mouth of man.

After the Eastern Question had sunk to rest,
during the last two years of Disraeli's rule, my

father had been immersed in the early life of Charles Fox. Happily preoccupied with that bygone world, he almost forgot modern politics ; even loud rumour from Midlothian was to him as the beating of a distant drum. In October 1879 he writes to his sister Alice :

My speeches have now at least the recommendation of rarity. I look forward to the time when I may again join the chorus who din and bewilder their fellow countrymen with ceaseless rhetoric.

And to his brother-in-law, Henry Holland, he wrote a few years later, reviewing his state of mind in the 'seventies :

The secret of my life is that I had a craving for literature, like that of some people for drink, and, till it was worked off, I could settle to nothing. Perhaps the most perfect simile would be that of a young man who is desperately in love, gets over it, and then goes about his business in peace afterwards.

He finished writing his Fox book just in time to enjoy the General Election of 1880. Fortune's wheel turned once more, spinning the more rapidly now that democracy had its hand thereon. My father's correspondence confirms much other evidence that the extent of the Conservative victory of 1874, and of the Liberal victory in 1880 both came as a surprise to politicians brought up under the more calculable electoral conditions of the middle century, when mass movements went for less and settled interests and influences for more. It is true that in 1868, the first election under the new franchise, he had made a calculation, just before the polls began, that proved exactly right as to the number of Liberals and of Conservatives who would be elected.[1] But the extent of the swing of the pendulum in 1874 and in 1880 surprised him as well as others.

'Fox' being ready for the press, he was fully prepared in April 1880 to enjoy and participate in the Liberal return to power. But Gladstone left him out of the Government. As usual, he wrote his feelings frankly to his sister Alice :

I am much hurt at the *manner* of leaving me out, though not much depressed or disappointed by the fact. But I am glad to find how very wide and deep the feeling about it is. Nowhere is it stronger than in the Government itself ; and under the pressure to do something, Gladstone, at the eleventh hour, in an ungracious manner, offered me to be under Chamberlain as Vice-President [of the Board of Trade].[2] He did not even say he thought I should do well to accept it, which I did not, and could not have done without political extinction. I am inclined to think that I am now in the position that suits me best, however unjustly I have been placed there. My book goes to Longman on the 1st of June. That means I can and shall give to politics all that for seven years has been bestowed on literature.

He had been a stalwart Gladstonian during the Eastern crisis, but that had not obliterated in

[1] The calculation lies before me—an interesting document. He has subscribed it: ' This was my calculation for the election of 1868, made out first with W. E. Forster, then with Lord Halifax, and finally revised by myself and signed on the 10th of November, two days before the polls opened. It was *exactly correct*.' He was always very proud of this prophecy, which argued a close knowledge of the political world of that day.

[2] As Chamberlain sat in the Commons, the Vice-President would not have had to answer for the Government in the House.

Gladstone's retentive mind his offence against the Church Schools of ten years back. The world in general was surprised and thought him ill treated. But he bore his disappointment with perfect good humour and dignity. The appearance and success of ' Fox ' further raised his reputation, and after a few months the Prime Minister thought good to make use of him again. In November 1880 he became Civil Lord of the Admiralty ; as his chief, Lord Northbrook, was in the Lords, he answered for the Admiralty in the Commons, and he was charged with the sort of administrative business that he liked. He wrote to Henry Sidgwick :

It is the post in the Ministry that I should prefer ; and to be appointed by Gladstone to a post of serious business straight from books is a protection against the sort of comments which the critical would make. My intense enjoyment of the work leads me to think that he sees the fact rightly, that I am not a literary politician, but a somewhat one-sided dogged personage who never cares for anything but his ends.

A letter to his sister Alice recalls the back-chat of the lobby that winter :

Our pipes have burst as usual, with the usual effect on the wall papers. I said to Dilke at the Speaker's dinner that I hoped there were other men there whose pipes had burst, and he said it was a fine instance of the very common motive which Bentham calls ' disinterested malevolence.' On Friday the Government was taken by surprise by the Irish giving over their obstruction, and there was no business to go on with. Harcourt said it was as when a horse runs away with you, and, when it stops short, you go over its head.

Meanwhile his 'Early History of Charles James Fox,' published in the autumn of 1880, had captivated the world of letters and politics. It was a biography of a totally different kind from the 'Life of Macaulay,' giving more satisfaction as a brilliant picture of a state of society than as the portrait of a statesman of whom nothing is there recorded except the years of his irresponsible boyhood and hardly less irresponsible youth. It is a work of historical art that has the effect of giving the reader the *entrée* as an intimate member of a bygone aristocratic society, which my father understood by tradition and sympathy better perhaps than any man of his time, certainly better than any man ever will again. It represents his peculiar habits of thought and style carried to their highest pitch. It is a *tour de force*. There is no other book quite of its kind, however that kind be rated.

The period of English life in which my father had taken a vigorous and joyful part had so far been peculiarly fortunate. It had been disturbed neither by war nor by any revolutionary movement; it had been prosperous alike in industry and agriculture; it had great leaders in every line of life; it was not unreasonably convinced of its own progress; its politics were neither too dull nor too bitter—one could write one's 'Ladies in Parliament' about them, light of heart. The problems that pressed for solution had in fact been dealt with in time by men of the stature of Disraeli and Gladstone, so that England was at peace within herself, mistress in her Empire, and safe from any ill effects of 'the envy of less happier lands.' It was not unnatural that shortly after the formation of the Government of 1880 my father should write to his sister Alice from abroad :

I am reading [Turgenief's] 'Fumée.' I think I never read a better-written novel, as far as I have got. It is astonishing what interest the Russians take in England and the English ; and why not ? For certainly we are far the first people in Europe, and, with the Americans, incomparably the first people in the world. As one gets older, and knows more of the world, one sees how so much that seemed so ordinary and commonplace around one implies a spread of energy and cultivation that must seem a perfect marvel to foreigners who can understand it.

These are not the words of a Jingo or of a man ignorant and contemptuous of foreigners. Yet even as he wrote them, clouds were beginning to gather on the edge of England's horizon. Her rural life, a necessary element in the health of any community, had just been stricken by that agricultural depression from which it has never recovered. Gladstone's new Government, come in to restore quiet where it was alleged that Beaconsfield had left disturbance, was already in deep trouble in South Africa and in Ireland. A revolutionary state of things had come into existence beyond St. George's Channel, destined to sway English politics out of their ordinary mild domestic courses for more than a generation to come, until the world-ruin of the Great War and

the class strife in England herself should render
her once proud inhabitants glad to get rid of
Ireland at almost any price.

When the new Parliament of 1880 assembled,
Parnell had two weapons in his hand to bring
England to what he regarded as reason—the Land
League in agrarian Ireland and Obstruction in
the House of Commons. Behind him and against
his authority was working a darker element of
crime. Gladstone endeavoured to meet the situation by a double policy of agrarian concession in
the form of Land Acts—duly mutilated by the
House of Lords—and coercion enforced by W. E.
Forster as Chief Secretary. Chamberlain and
Morley opposed the policy of coercion, and
Gladstone himself was uneasy at the wholesale
imprisonment of men merely on suspicion.
Forster declared that if he could lock up a
calculable number of ' village ruffians,' he could
govern Ireland. He tried bravely and honestly,
and he failed. With Parnell in prison, lawless-
ness was freed from the partial constraint of his
control. Gladstone saw that Forster's policy was
bankrupt. He let Parnell out of prison and gave
orders for a milder regime. Forster resigned,
and his place as Chief Secretary was taken by
Lord Frederick Cavendish, Gladstone's relation
by marriage and personal friend, sent over as the
harbinger of peace, a noble warrant of England's
desire for new and better things.

On May 6, 1882, Lord Frederick landed in
Ireland, passed through Dublin, met Mr. Burke,

the permanent Under-Secretary, and in his company began to walk across the Phœnix Park towards his new home, the Chief Secretary's Lodge. The two were waylaid and murdered with knives by the roadside. The assassins were the 'Invincibles,' a small murder club, averse to Parnell's policy, which indeed they struck hard that day. Parnell's authority in Ireland and influence in England never quite recovered the blow. And the memory of Lord Frederick's murder became one of the chief impediments in the path of Gladstone, when a few years later he tried to persuade the English to trust the Irish with self-government. My father, who knew Frederick Cavendish and his wife so well, always declared that such was his influence on Gladstone and such his strong good sense, that, if he had lived, the break-up of the Liberal party in 1886 would not have taken place.

Whatever men, parties and nations may have suffered in years to come from that bloody stab, the news of it struck first and hardest the noble lady, Gladstone's niece, my father's confidant and friend in his troubles of fifteen years before. Twelve months after the fatal day, Lady Frederick Cavendish wrote to him at the Lodge in the Phœnix :

I am more touched by far by hearing of those simple crosses of small stones laid on the spot by unknown hands, and evidently respected by all, than I could have been by any regular monument there that might have caused painful, bitter or antagonistic feelings.

She survived her husband forty-three years. She became a strong supporter of Home Rule for Ireland. Her Diary of the years 1862 to 1882, published after her death by John Bailey, leaves to posterity the picture of that part of her beautiful life which had been lived in the sun of social pleasures and domestic happiness. The book became my father's favourite reading during the last year of his own life, recalling to him the past in a way that he seemed to prefer to every other.

In May 1882 Mr. Gladstone offered him the place vacated by Lord Frederick's death. In the circumstances a man of spirit could hardly refuse, and he was moreover glad to serve under Lord Spencer and help him to save from the wreck all that was still practicable of the policy of conciliation.

It was a tragic week. Five days after the assassination, while my father was making his first hasty journey to Ireland, his sister Alice's husband, Stratford Dugdale, lay dying, the victim of his own generous courage in hastening to the rescue of colliers entombed by an accident in his Warwickshire mine. In spite of the general pre-occupation with the Phœnix Park murders, Dugdale's heroic death took the imagination of Englishmen. Gladstone said to my father that such deeds as Dugdale's gave him hope for the country. It was a strange coincidence that the week of his sister's life when my father would have most wished to be near her, was the week in his life when imperative duty called him elsewhere.

My own darling Alice,

It is heart-rending to think of your grief, and of my
enforced absence. I never felt anything so much. The
state of the country here is very sad ; but you must not
think of me as in actual danger. The question is one of
precaution and no device is neglected. It was a very
different risk that made your husband's death so truly
glorious. They feel very much for you at the Viceregal
Lodge, where I am now staying. Could it be inserted in
the account that I was detained here, and how deeply I
regret it ?

Lord Spencer was his chief, but it was he who
answered for Ireland in the House of Commons,
facing the venom and the wit of the Parnellite
opposition. All-night sittings and racial antagon-
isms on the floor of the House are wearing things,
and he was once so provoked as to remind the
Celtic bull-baiters that ' though he might be an
Irish Secretary he was still an English gentleman.'
But, truth to tell, they and he had a kind of
human fellow-feeling behind it all. In August
1883 he wrote to his sister Alice :

Somehow or other, the Irish members have a strange
and almost ineradicable liking for me. Healy the other
day talked of me as singularly courteous and genial,
' and this,' he said, ' though I do not forget the Richmond
incident,' which meant that I had put him in prison for
four months out of the last five.

Forty years on, when the tide of time had
floated Healy into the Vice-Regal Lodge as
Governor-General of the Irish Free State, he and

my father exchanged friendly correspondence
about those old days.

But the crux of the matter lay not at Westminster
but in Ireland. The state of things with which
Lord Spencer and his Chief Secretary had to cope
in the months following the Phœnix Park murders
has been described by John Morley, himself not
without experience of Irish government, as ' a
society on the eve of dissolution.'

The Invincibles still roved with knives about the streets
of Dublin. Discontent had been stirred in the ranks of
the Royal Irish Constabulary, and a dangerous mutiny
broke out in the metropolitan force. Over half the
country the demoralization of every class, the terror, the
fierce hatred, the universal distrust, had grown to an
incredible pitch. The new viceroy attacked the formidable task before him with resolution, minute assiduity,
and an inexhaustible store of that steady-eyed patience
which is the sovereign requisite of any man who, whether
with coercion or without, takes in hand to govern Ireland.
He was seconded with high ability and courage by
Mr. Trevelyan, whose fortitude was subjected to a far
severer trial than has ever fallen to the lot of any Irish
Secretary before or since [1903].[1]

My father's devotion to the ' Red Earl ' was
life-long. It was based on admiration of Lord
Spencer's strong, slow, silent, benevolent wisdom,
at once liberal and aristocratic, akin to that displayed by his uncle Lord Althorp in steering the
great Reform Bill through the Commons. The
Viceroy and the Secretary trusted each other
completely and were in complete agreement.

[1] *Life of Gladstone* (Morley), Book VIII, chap. iv.

Almost every day that they were not together they wrote to one another on business, as their extant correspondence shows. They were determined not to revert to Forster's measures or to their spirit, nor to slide into military rule, nor to become the partisans of the Orangemen, and yet they were determined to maintain, or rather to restore, law and order in Ireland. In this they succeeded. But they neither of them deceived themselves into supposing, as successful administrators are in such circumstances often tempted to suppose, that they had ' solved the problem ' of Ireland.

In August 1882, when the very worst was over, the Chief Secretary after a tour in Ulster wrote to his sister Alice from the Phœnix :

Belfast was a very thriving place, and it was pleasant to find, all through Ulster, that both parties seemed equally kindly affected towards the present Irish Government. We are going to begin entertaining people at the end of this week, and I suppose it will then never end. Things are mending here, fast and surely, as far as crime and disorder in general are concerned, though I fancy that there is more probability than ever of some sensational crime. It is an odd atmosphere to find oneself in : and very unlike what I should have chosen for myself. The little boys are very happy, and Carry tolerates it. It is her way always to take things as she finds them. The garden and grounds are beautiful.

My elder brothers were in Ireland only for their school holidays, but I, being six years old, was still at home. I spent much of my time wandering round the wooded circle of the Chief Secretary's

The Chief Secretary with his Family, outside his Lodge in the Phœnix,

grounds, playing at marbles and hide-and-seek with a mild and gigantic Irish plain-clothes detective, named Mr. Dunne, whom I regarded as my playmate, and who was incidentally responsible for the preservation of my small person. It was startling to discover one day that he took the opposite side about the battle of the Boyne. There were frequent reviews of real red and blue soldiers—cavalry, infantry and artillery— who fired at each other, and advanced and re- treated with entrancing jangle and rattle across the open Phœnix ; our grounds were like a private box for viewing these delights.

Unconsciously a sense of the drama of English and Irish history was purveyed to me through daily sights and experiences, with my father as commentator and bard. On a great beech tree on the lawn was carved an ancient caricature of the Duke of Wellington, who, as his successor loved to remember, had once on a time been Chief Secretary. How a general could be a Chief Secretary remained to me one of the insoluble mysteries that childhood learns to accept. The love of history, and above all of military history, was deeply and affectionately planted in me while living thus, a queer, happy little boy, almost alone with my parents in this oasis in the surrounding prairie of the Phœnix. They were gala days when my father found time to come up to my room and teach me the arcana of an elaborate family tradition with regard to the proper use of several hundred small lead soldiers, my brothers' delight in the holidays and mine all the year round. In October 1882 he writes to his sister Alice :

I have just contrived to set George playing at a ' City ' instead of those eternal battles.   It reminded me so of old days [1] ; except that his games are one continual revolution, in which the roughs, the police, the students of the University, the tradesmen and the ' gents ' form different combinations, and always end by killing the whole of each other.   He has no idea of the quiet flow of civil life. I am glad to say that there are slight indications that Ireland is beginning to return to a state of things less resembling that of George's town.

Be it understood, however, by the uninitiated that ' those eternal battles ' were in fact the serious part of the affair, and grew in later years at Wallington into a scientific but picturesque *kriegspiel*, played over the uncarpeted floor of a large room by my brothers and myself with several thousands of little lead soldiers.   It was my father who started us all on this thrilling occupation—I am not certain whether to call it an art or a science.

In January 1884, when he was nearing the end of his Secretaryship, he writes to his sister Alice :

I hardly know what to write of Irish affairs.   They seem to be capable of only one attitude of mind : silent endurance.   Forster found them unendurable because of his higher qualities, which rendered it intolerable to him

---

[1] Since my father in his childhood and boyhood had been the playmate of his sister Alice, civilian and domestic life had played a larger though not a predominant part in their imaginings and games with the little lead men. Macaulay had not seldom lent a hand.

to work in so hopeless and thankless an element. I get along because I regard it in a dogged, semi-sulky way, as if one had to walk uphill against the rain and wind, in a fog, for an indefinite number of miles, being certain of nothing except that you are walking in what you *believe* to be the right direction, and renouncing all idea of finding pleasure in the landscape. I feel no more inclined to throw up the job than I did a year ago. If good does not come out of our endeavours, one hopes that they will result in a minimum of harm.

A month before he had written to his sister Margaret :

The effect of getting used to what is bad in Ireland is that you get more and more disgusted with the whole thing. The perversity of everybody who either writes or speaks is something inconceivable. If these people were left to themselves, we should have a mutual massacre ; unless they are not quite as brave as they pretend.

It is easy to understand why, two years later, he had doubts about Gladstone's Home Rule.

Whether the experience aged him in any important sense I am not certain. It is true that his hair and beard began to turn white during his Irish Secretaryship, a circumstance much commented upon. He was only forty-six, but hair as black as his often grizzles early. Before he left his post, peace and order had been temporarily restored, without resort to abnormal or violent methods.

In October 1884 he had his due reward and became a Cabinet Minister, as Chancellor of the Duchy of Lancaster, an office ' without portfolio,' very desirable as an honourable sofa to rest upon for awhile. He used always to boast that as Chancellor of the Duchy he appointed the first working man who ever became a J.P. in England.

In the winter of 1884–5 the County Franchise Bill, embodying the reform he had done so much to bring forward, was passed, after much agitation. A quarrel with the Lords on the time-relation of the Franchise and the Redistribution Bills was appeased with the help of the Queen as mediator. According to her journal of October 29, 1884, she had been moved to play that rôle with such vigour and success, in part by the representations made to her by my father as to the dangers, in the then state of England and Ireland, of a dissolution of Parliament and a General Election on the Lords and Franchise question. She added, ' Mr. Trevelyan I find very agreeable and sensible, and not a violent Radical, as he used to be.' [1]

My father presented Mr. Gladstone with a medallion of Fox by Tassie, to commemorate the passing of the County Franchise Act. His relations with his chief were now excellent. The Grand Old Man thanked him for the little present in the following words :

Jan. 24, 1885.

My dear Trevelyan,

Accept my hearty thanks for your gift, most interesting in itself, and for the occasion with which in words of so much kindness you have connected it. If there has been anything special to myself in the recent satisfactory

---

[1] Buckle, *Queen's Letters* (2nd series), iii. pp. 561, 565.

arrangement with regard to the Representation of the People, I really believe it has been due to that disposition of the country to confide in and defer to old age, which (as I consider) is entertained out of doors in excess, but which may on occasion be turned to good account.

The writer was destined ere long to put this ' disposition ' to a very severe test. On December 29, 1885, my father wrote to his sister Alice :

It is the Grand Old Man's birthday ! He seems to make more noise in the world, the older he gets.

In the following year the noise was to become much louder than ever before.

CHAPTER V

HOME RULE POLITICS, 1886–1897. COUNTRY LIFE IN NORTHUMBERLAND. RETIREMENT FROM POLITICS. 'THE AMERICAN REVOLUTION.' ROOSEVELT AND OTHER FRIENDS. THE WAR. THE END

IN the Parliament that sat from 1880 to 1885 the Irish Nationalists had been, for the first time, a great force in English politics. In the next Parliament, elected under the new County Franchise, they were the dominating factor; their eighty-five votes, holding the balance between Conservative and Liberal, were a weapon in Parnell's hand, wielded to extort Home Rule without remorse or regard for any English interest. Under the terms of Pitt's Union, Ireland could, if she so determined, render the Parliamentary government of England impossible. She had now so determined. The end of the old system was at hand; the only question was how soon and on what terms it would be wound up. If men had been wise, English Conservatives and Liberals would have taken counsel together how to solve this Imperial problem. But nations only learn wisdom when they have suffered for many years, and not always then. Our post-war generation will probably wonder why these grand Victorian statesmen did not do the obvious thing—grant Home Rule to Ireland excluding Ulster. But such a *pis-aller* was not even considered. In that age of optimists no one, Unionist or Home Ruler, would allow that an arrangement which did not pretend to attain perfection might conceivably be the truest wisdom. The unity of Ireland was, most fatally, regarded by both sides as axiomatic. Our two-party system appeared at its worst in dealing with the Irish question, which it attempted to solve by raising the political atmosphere to boiling point.

As the first result of the General Election of December 1885 Gladstone had formed a new Ministry. It was understood that some sort of political devolution was to take place in Ireland, and partly for this reason Lord Hartington, the representative of the old Whig aristocratic element in the party, refused to join the Government. Chamberlain and my father took office, hoping to be able to agree to the ultimate form that the Irish measure would take when it had been ' knocked about in the Cabinet.'

My father became Secretary for Scotland, a post that suited him well. He introduced a Crofters' Bill, to deal with the agrarian grievances of the Scottish Highland tenantry. They were curiously analogous to those of the Irish peasant,[1]

---

[1] The landlord did not, as in England and southern Scotland, erect and maintain the buildings, etc. The story is well known of the crofter giving evidence before the Commission. ' Did you put up the house ? Aye, I put up the hoose. And did you put up the walls ? Aye, I put up the walls. And what did the landlord put up ? He put up the rent ! '

but without the added complication of religious and racial feud between farmer and landlord. The same principles as had been applied to Ireland by the recent Land Acts—fixity of tenure and fair rents adjudicated by a Commission—were applied to the Scottish Highlands by the Crofters' Act and went far towards solving the problem. But my father had to hand over his measure to others to carry through its later stages, for at the end of March 1886 he resigned office. He left the Cabinet with Chamberlain, from inability to agree to the principle of complete Home Rule. He also objected to the accompanying scheme of Land Purchase.

In April 1886 the Home Rule Bill was introduced into the House of Commons, and after two months of anxious lobbying and debate was thrown out owing to the large Liberal Unionist vote. Gladstone was faced with the choice between dissolution or resignation. To resign meant postponement, a waiting on time and events, an attempt at reconciliation within the Liberal party before it was too late. To dissolve would force the Liberal Unionists to fight against their old friends and to be returned by Conservative votes. It would be the end of the old Liberal party. It would make impossible all attempts to settle the Irish question by agreement. It would compel Conservatives and Liberal Unionists to exploit the Englishman's natural contempt and dislike for the Irish race. For these reasons my father thought that Gladstone's decision in the summer of 1886 to go to the country on the Home Rule issue, instead of sending in his resignation, was a profound and irretrievable mistake ; and he never ceased to think so even after he had decided to rejoin and fight under his banner, as the less bad of the two alternatives to which politicians were now reduced.

In this unhappy General Election of 1886 he stood as a Liberal Unionist, and was defeated at the Border Burghs. It was the end of a very pleasant connection of nearly twenty years. But his defeat was a blessing in disguise, partly because his father's death that summer and the changes it involved gave him much to do out of Parliament, and partly because election as a Liberal Unionist would have landed him in a false position. Angry as he was with Gladstone, he found that it was not in his nature to be at ease in the Conservative camp. The violence of upper class reaction against the Liberals, the common abuse of our Irish fellow subjects employed as political stock-in-trade, the nascent ' Imperialism ' of the revived Tory party, all these were more distasteful to him than Home Rule and the increased Radicalism of the Gladstonian Liberals.

The Imperialism of that epoch, which became the inspiration of the Conservative-Unionist alliance under Salisbury and Chamberlain, had many merits, but it had very serious faults which were peculiarly repugnant to my father. In particular he was alienated by the dislike or contempt which it engendered of Irishman, Indian and Boer, and of all constituents of the Empire that were not Anglo-Saxon. His intimate correspondence with his sister Alice shows, no less clearly than his public utterances, why he moved back to the Gladstonian camp. Not that he loved Cæsar more, but that he loved his enemies less.

Dec. 23, 1887.

I am shocked at the brutal attack on the Irish members at the Westminster Play. It is a shame to bring boys up with such feelings. The fact is that hatred of the Irish is the one good card the Tories have, and they must work it. But where can it lead them? They must go forward, for the nature of hatred is that it grows hotter unless the causes are removed.

Dec. 3, 1888.

I was much shocked at Salisbury's allusion to the ' black man,' and his excusing it by announcing that he did not know whether natives of India were black or not. But I suppose he knows the people whom he is addressing.

My father was so made that he was always certain to take a side. There was very little philosophic doubt in his composition. He became a Home Ruler, and as early as July 1887 stood at a by-election for the Bridgeton Division of Glasgow and was returned to Parliament. He sat for Bridgeton until he retired from politics ten years later.

In these circumstances it was inevitable that he should be hotly attacked, that he should be called the ' political weather-cock,' and made to eat his words. Chamberlain, the greatest master of political onslaught in that era of heavy hitting, turned upon him with acrimony, after their paths, which had for a few months run together, sharply and suddenly ran apart. In taking his decision to stand for Glasgow, he wrote to his sister Alice :

The violence of the Liberal Unionist papers is scandalous. Far worse than the Conservative. I am very glad that we are going to fight it out. Ever since I said that the Liberal party ought to be reconciled, they have been abusing me ; and they may just as well have something to abuse me for.

If my father had remained out of the fray from 1886 onwards, no one would have blamed him and he would thenceforth have led an altogether delectable existence, such as in fact he led from the time of his retirement in 1897 till his death—writing books at Wallington. But it was no ignoble impulse that sent him back for another decade among the gladiators, with the prospect of collecting more dust than laurels.

Nam neque nos agere hoc patriaï tempore iniquo
Possumus aequo animo.

To his sister Alice :

Feb. 16, 1889.

I have determined to go straight ahead, and make myself as formidable, and contribute to make the party as formidable as I can. In this world ideas and opinions get justice in proportion as they are strongly held, and, in the long run, they are strongly held in proportion as they are right and just.

Such was his philosophy of action. I trust that it is as true as it is invigorating and useful.

Many old friendships were being broken. The intellectual and literary society of London and the Universities in which he had lived and moved all his life had been mainly Liberal ; it now became mainly Unionist, nourishing hot detestation of Gladstone and moral reprobation of his followers. But the friendships for which he cared most of all, especially those of Henry Sidgwick and Edward Bowen, were unaffected by political difference. And a fair proportion of his old friends, like Arthur Sidgwick, Henry Jackson and Harry Thompson, still followed the Gladstonian banner into fresh fields under a lowering sky. Nor was my father one with whom any lover of history or letters found it easy to quarrel : strong Unionists like Lecky, Arthur Elliot, Jebb, and Harry Holland, Lord Knutsford, his well-beloved brother-in-law, were glad to get away with him and talk about other things than our unhappy politics. I remember many pleasant visits that such men paid to him at his country homes. There too were to be found his non-political friends, Sir Garnet Wolseley, to whom he was drawn by a common love of military history and the soldier's fundamental liberality of mind ; and Henry James of the orbed forehead, holding his hearers wrapt in joyous anticipation, while he sought magisterially for the one right word that was to act as corner-stone to the suspended sentence. The society of such men as these—besides his own colleagues the Gladstonian lieutenants, Rosebery, Harcourt, Kimberley, Morley, Bryce, and, among

the younger generation, his Northumbrian neigh-
bour, Sir Edward Grey—would console any
reasonable being for the fact that politics had
become more hot and more futile than of old.
After his final retirement he wrote to Roosevelt :

For ten years [1887–1897] I sat next Morley in the
House of Commons, and it was a great antidote to the
dreariness and bad rhetoric which was the prevailing
atmosphere of that, as, I suppose, of all National Assem-
blies. I thought him and Henry Sidgwick the most delightful company of our generation ; and Sidgwick is gone.

His personal relations with Gladstone during
the last period were good, though never intimate.
To Roosevelt he writes again in 1905 in reminiscent
mood :

Our generation in England was curiously affected by
the question of age. Mr. Gladstone, in gifts and faculties,
was exactly a whole generation better than his time of
life ; and, while the Liberal party in some respects gained
by it, it in some respects was damaged. In his later years
he sometimes retained in important offices old colleagues
who, though they were actually his juniors, were entirely
worn out ; and it was noticeable how certain clever men
and ambitious outsiders were thrown into very unfortunate
political courses by the sense of being overshadowed by
him, and by not being favourites with him. When John
Morley, and Bryce, and I were men of fifty, he was old
enough, and more, to be our father ; and he regarded us
with great indulgence—at times even to the verge of
spoiling us—as so many promising sons. We certainly
were very fond of him. But I cannot help wishing that
he had retired from office long before he did, and had
allowed the Liberal party to work out its own salvation,
make its own mistakes, and learn from its own experience.

My father always regarded himself as the most fortunate of beings, and was ever ready to ' count his mercies.' Politics, he used to say, had become ' detestable,' and London society no longer entirely pleasant, but at this very point in time the most delightful country life in the world became his in the fullest measure. The Wallington estate in Northumberland came to him by his father's death in 1886, and the Welcombe estate near Stratford-on-Avon came to my mother by the death of her father Robert Philips in 1890.[1]

Even before our two grandfathers had died, we boys had come to regard these two delectable places as our holiday homes—broad Northumberland for the summer, and Warwickshire for Christmas feasting presided over by our almost too hospitable grandpapa, Robert Philips. Having been a hearty Liberal all his life, he died an equally hearty Unionist, but he took no shadow of objection to my father for going his own way in the matter. I remember him still, lying goutily in his great leather chair in the great panelled hall, while *The Times* leading article of the day was read to him, its fulminations against Parnell and Gladstone endorsed and punctuated by his outbursts. He swore in an old-fashioned, full-blooded, entirely genial manner. His rough benevolence of soul gave me an idea of the older English character, now passed away. My father appreciated him in the highest degree. The

[1] His elder brother, Mark Philips (see pp. 79, 86, above), had died in December 1873, having proved, as he had promised, a good uncle to his niece and the husband she had chosen in his despite.

Welcombe estate, which my mother inherited on his death, had been administered by him in a manner entirely his own ; my father had written in the 'seventies :

It is very funny to see the Pater's Liberal views coming out in his dealings with the tenants and poor folk on the estate. He treats them just as he does the Lancashire people : as independent people with a standing of their own, and yet everything is perfectly managed.

He was buried at his favourite place of worship, the Unitarian chapel at Stand, near Prestwich, Manchester. The old family mansion and grounds hard by, known as The Park, now a most interesting monument of the ways of life of Manchester merchant princes a century and more ago, went on his death to my aunt Anna Philips. Thenceforth she often paid long visits to my parents ; her devotion to my mother and thoughtful care of my father in his later years formed an important and most happy feature of their lives to the end.

After Welcombe, in 1890, had come into my mother's possession, she and my father used it as a winter resort, living, and entertaining their guests, in the smaller half of the too vast mansion, which appears from the hill above like a village of red brick. It is now a hotel, frequented by Americans on pilgrimage to Shakespeare's shrine a mile off along the footpath way. They follow the trail of Theodore Roosevelt, Ambassador Choate and others of their fellow-countrymen who stayed with my parents at Welcombe. For its present purpose it is, I understand, regarded, for the first time in its existence, as too small !

But our real home was Wallington in Northumberland, and the long summer holidays there were the best part of our lives. The death of my grandfather Sir Charles Trevelyan in 1886 left my father to be Baronet and squire of Wallington for no less than forty-two years. He has described the house, in which he lived so happily and so long, in two articles written for the well-known series in *Country Life* (June 22 and 29, 1918).

The present house was built in William III's reign by the Tyneside magnate, Sir William Blackett ; he had bought the estate and the old castle of Wallington from Sir John Fenwick, who had run through his money under the Merry Monarch, before ever he took to the paths of Jacobite conspiracy which led him to the block. My father writes to Roosevelt :

This place was a seat of Sir John Fenwick. A few years before his Act of Attainder Wallington was bought by my great grandfather's great grandfather, Sir William Blackett, from Sir John Fenwick ; a principal part of the purchase money being an annuity on Sir John Fenwick's life of 2,000 pounds a year. Blackett pulled down the castle and built the house I live in. He was a famous Whig and (I suppose) voted in every division with his party on Fenwick's Bill of Attainder. But I hope not.

Sir William Blackett had begun to build the new Wallington in the year of the Revolution. But the much admired Italian decorations of the interior of the house, the giant beech woods, the

THE EIGHTEENTH-CENTURY GARDEN AT WALLINGTON.

garden designed by Capability Brown,[1] the farms,
roads, and enclosures that turned the region from
a moorland to a centre of rural civilisation, were
due to Sir Walter Blackett, one of the greatest
improving landlords of the mid-eighteenth century.
Rural Northumberland owes much of its charm
and prosperity to the money that the Tyneside
magnates of that fortunate era made in mines and
commerce, and lavished with equal munificence
and taste on the countryside they adored.

It can well be imagined how my father enjoyed
such a place and its history. The rough shooting
on the heather and white-grass moors was just to
his liking. He had shot a great deal in Whig
country houses in the first half of his life, but
henceforth he found full occupation for the sportsman's year on his own land. Besides a sufficiency
of grouse, partridges and pheasants, there was then
abundance of blackgame, of which he notes that we
shot over two hundred cocks one year. But since
those days the blackcock have ' dwindled long by
slow decay,' at Wallington as elsewhere. Besides
regular days of shooting, he loved ' poking about
with a gun.' ' I shot a duck this morning,' he
writes, ' which always delights me more than
anything except winning an election.' And on
another occasion : ' Wild ducks are a fascinating
quarry, for they are such true wild animals, coming

---

[1] ' Capability ' Brown, who introduced landscape gardening and abolished
the artificial Dutch garden, was a native of Cambo, the village of the Wallington estate. His fame became national, if not international. He was
called ' Capability ' Brown not because of his own capability, great as it was,
but because when taken to see a nobleman's or gentleman's grounds, after
looking round he would say, ' I see great *capability* for improvement here.'

from one knows not where, and certainly not lending themselves to capture.' And again : ' In the afternoons I walk in the snow with a gun, like a man in the vignette in Bewick, but I hardly hit anything and see little.'

Of the delights of his country home none meant more to him than the books. During two centuries of family history, innumerable volumes once belonging to Fenwicks, Calverleys, Blacketts, Macaulays and Trevelyans had drifted together at Wallington. It was his part, by selection, rejection and addition, to weld them into one most readable country-house library. When he had made it, he settled down to live in it for the rest of his life, reading a much greater proportion of his books than most owners of country-house collections. In June 1887, the year of his absence from Parliament and his first year as owner of Wallington, he writes to his sister Alice :

We are extremely busy fitting up the house, which requires a good deal to complete it. Especially I have been spending an immense deal of time over the books, of which we had a vast collection of ancient Macaulay— many Zachary Macaulay—books. One sees that, one time or another, somebody must have wrestled with every old country house library. It has been very lucky just now having plenty of time on my hands.

He was a great reader aloud, to my mother alone, and to all of us on the holidays.

To his sister Alice :

Jan. 11, 1888.

We are winding up our shooting and our intellectual occupations. We have read ' Persuasion ' aloud. The scene of Captain Wentworth writing the letter is absolutely perfect. On the whole, I like it the best of the lot—even of that lot.

June 6, 1888.

I have just finished Peacock's 'Maid Marian,' 'Crotchet Castle,' 'Nightmare Abbey' and 'Headlong Hall.' I am so glad that I put them off till now. They require most minute reading, and repay you with infinite laughter and much poetry and wisdom.

Jan. 22, 1889.

I have been reading the Life of my uncle out loud to the boys. The feeling of our respective families about him is the most curious instance of family 'solidarity' that I know. It is certain that, in 1930, there will be several men with a lively personal feeling of affection towards a man who was born in 1800 !

Margaret, Lady Knutsford, retained just the same feeling about her uncle as her brother George and her sister Alice. In January 1899 she writes to my father :

I went to-day to the Abbey, as I do every year at the time when the Dean kindly allows the stone to be uncovered for a week, to lay my wreaths on it. Meta's three elder children went with me and each brought a wreath to lay on, and it touched me to see the three little great great nephews and niece laying them on, and so deeply interested and excited about it.

My father was fortunate in both his sisters. If Alice was more nearly of his age, and the more constant recipient of his confidences from child-hood upwards, the elder sister, Margaret, had an old-world dignity and beauty of speech and character which exerted over him a powerful charm.

To Roosevelt he writes in 1906 :

I look up to you as a reader of Milton's prose. I never have taken to Sixteenth or Seventeenth Century prose ; but I may some day ; for I never read Chaucer till three years ago, and I have since read him [viz. the Tales] twice through aloud, and he has spoiled me for any other poetry. . . . Have you got ' Sponge's Sporting Tour ' ? Many years ago I had a bad typhoid fever ; and, as then was the custom, it was concealed from me what was the matter with me. But I gradually lost all interest in books, and in most other human beings ; when suddenly there came on me a craving to read ' Sponge,' which I had read a dozen times, and have read several times since ; and I even then read it with delight. I never understand how ' Jorrocks ' can be placed on a level with it. Macaulay— whose knowledge of a horse was confined to a pretty clear recognition of the difference between its head and its tail —was much interested in ' Sponge.'

' Yes,' is the reply, ' Mrs. Roosevelt and I are both as fond as you are of the immortal " Soapy Sponge." '

My father's tastes in reading, though mainly retrospective, were by no means so altogether. He was a very early admirer of Stevenson, Meredith, Rudyard Kipling and the great American novelists of that era, and he delighted in a London Irish author who was bringing out obscure novels in the 'eighties entitled ' Cashel Byron's Profession ' and the ' Unsocial Socialist.' He admired Samuel Butler's books when to do so was rare, but lived to be annoyed at the vogue of extreme Butler-worship. As the twentieth century advanced he was a keen and discriminating patron of its novelists. But his reading was chiefly in the past, and as time went by more and more in the Greek and Latin authors. In the last years of his life he kept a list of his reading which would have done credit to a scholar intent on a first in the Classical Tripos.

He early established with me a camaraderie of nonsense, mainly of the literary and historical order. He began it before I went to school, and it was still going on when I was at College :

June 5, 1896.

Dear George,

I am glad that your last day [of the Tripos] has come : I felt more *en train* on the Saturday than all the rest of the week.

> Keep up your pecker
> Like brave Madame Necker,
> Who as Mademoiselle Curchod,
> Instead of making a poor show,
> (When her swain cut and run
> And ' obeyed as a son ')
> Just tripped up her anchor
> And caught a rich banker.

Charles and I have been playing billiards but only so so : the gunroom has not been a cannon-room to any great extent. Rain has come at last, and I shall fish this afternoon, so as to be able to swagger about it in the lobby next week.

May 17, 1894.

Dear George,

If you have not read ' Boswelliana ' you should read it from cover to cover. It tells you more of the man than anything else. We have a copy in both our houses. Whatever Macaulay's crimes against Boswell are, by this time he has expiated them. I have no doubt that for 35 years Boswell has been putting his head between him and Milman and Thirlwall whenever he saw them together. I always think Macaulay's article in the ' Encyclopædia Britannica ' on Johnson, as compared with the Review in the *Edinburgh*, a splendid specimen of a writer who gained by growing old and so far had lost nothing.

Journeys abroad with him were an historical education of the most delightful kind. He had the quality of making his companion feel the excitement that he himself felt at being privileged to see the battlefield af Waterloo, or the staircase in the tragic house at Delft at the foot of which William the Silent was murdered, or the places where the Tuileries, the guillotine and Salle de Manége once stood ; and as to the Forum, the Palatine, the Campagna, they were holy ground, where history's most royal pageant had been played. I have been with many wonderful cicerones, including Lanciani and Boni, but in his own way he was unequalled. I do not know, but perhaps the present generation cannot be expected to feel such excitement in seeing spots where old murders and battles and revolutions were enacted ; we have supped so full of horrors ourselves, and Europe has been so freshly washed in seas of blood.

> The world is weary of the past.
> Oh, might it die, or rest at last !

But at the end of the Victorian era, for an Englishman at least, those

> Old unhappy far-off things
> And battles long ago

had a charm which my father's eager reverence, tempered with the usual jokes of allusion, made more actual than the rather uninspiring present. On one of these occasions he took me up to see the Janiculum, partly for the view's sake, partly for Lars Porsena's sake, more for the sake of Garibaldi. There, on the spot, among the vineyards that then lay around the Porta San Pancrazio, he told me the story of Garibaldi's defence of the Roman Republic, which I had never heard of before. Another day we went to Shelley's grave ; the two places seemed to have a spiritual connection, answering to their similar positions, each beside one of the more remote gates of Rome.

From 1892 to 1895 the Liberals were again in office with the help of the Irish vote. Gladstone made my father Secretary for Scotland once more, a post he filled with pleasure to himself, and, so far as I can learn, with satisfaction to the Scots. The quiescence of their affairs was in strange contrast to the violently controversial character of everything Irish. Indeed my father's chief administrative trouble, if such it can be called, arose from the deep interest Queen Victoria took in things Scottish, and her definite views as to Crown appointments, especially of Professors of

Philosophy ! I was brought up at home to regard Queen Victoria with immense respect—' a very great lady ' my father used to say in his emphatic manner—but not as the absolute perfection of human wisdom, any more than Mr. Gladstone himself.

In 1895 he regained the freedom of opposition without a sigh. ' One likes being turned out better than being put in,' he wrote to his sister Alice. Perhaps elderly statesmen more often feel like that than the world wots of. Two years later he resigned his seat in the House, and from 1897 to his death in 1928 he was out of politics altogether.

He had been a fine and popular platform speaker, and his prepared speeches in the House had been greatly appreciated for the clear, bell-like quality of his voice and the literary finish of his phrases and images. But the quality that leads to the very highest places in our commonwealth, the power of impromptu debate, had not been his strongest point. As a colleague and an administrator he was never found wanting.

As his farewell to the political scene I will quote the letter that he wrote to his sister Alice in May 1898, after taking part in Gladstone's funeral at Westminster Abbey. His own somewhat chequered relations with the departed hero give interest to his testimony :

It was by far the finest and noblest thing I ever saw or read of. One thing came home to one—the transitoriness of calumny. Mr. Gladstone made his mistakes—but in so fierce a career one now sees that all that is unavoidable.

SIR GEORGE TREVELYAN

outside Wallington.

Lesser men, one and all, make as many in proportion. But ever since I came to London, as long as he was in affairs, there was frequent, insolent and almost brutal conduct in the House, and in society continuous talk about his being bad, absurd, a Jesuit, a madman, moved only by his own interests, a hypocrite—what not? And the lighter, but almost most offensive weapons were largely directed against Mrs. G. And now, where is it all? The *personal* estimate is unanimous, among those who are capable of making an estimate at all. And Lord Salisbury (a better judge than Randolph Churchill and Drummond Wolff who would have it that he was an Atheist) solemnly pronounces him, once for all, as the greatest Christian among public men. What an example! For it is the example of a man of the world, not only of like passions, but with like difficulties and impossibilities as others.

When my father retired from politics it was generally wished and expected that he would finish his 'Life of Charles James Fox.' It had long been a saying among his friends that there ought to be an Act of Parliament to compel him to do so ; and to this day it is common for his English admirers to regret that he left it undone to write instead the history of the American Revolution.[1] Nor indeed is it likely that anyone will ever again know and love the society of which Fox was the moving spirit as my father knew and loved it, or that anyone will again be in such complete sympathy both with that lost, delightful

[1] The *American Revolution* came out in the following parts over a period of fifteen years : Part I (1766–1776), 1899 ; II, 2 vols, 1903 ; III, 1907 ; *George III and Charles Fox*, the concluding part of the *American Revolution*, vol. i, 1912, vol. ii, 1914.

world, so aristocratic and so English, and also with the democratic views that Fox developed in the last twenty years of his life. Those views are Fox's real contribution to the development of English political life, for the attitude which he took up after the French Revolution, however much open to censure from certain important points of view, sowed the seeds of later development of the Whig into the Liberal party, and enabled Reform to come without Revolution a generation after he himself had been laid in the grave. All these things my father might have made so vivid and so clear if he had been content to work in the protected arena of a Life of Fox. Confined within those limits and enjoying the chartered privileges of biography, his work would have been less open to challenge than it is in his history of the American Revolution.

Yet there is another side to the question—to wit the other side of the Atlantic. It is true that the book, though not ill received in England, has failed to become permanently popular over here, for the story of the loss of the American colonies can never be grateful to English ears, and many think his narrative too favourable to the Americans. On the other hand the book has had a great effect in the United States, where its chief sale has always been. It did much to help the movement over there for a better understanding of England. It emphasised the strong element of opposition that existed in England to the policy of George III, it disposed of many anti-English myths current on the other side of the Atlantic, and above all it represented the English life and people of that day in a pleasanter and more intimate light than any to which American readers were accustomed. He did a work of no small value by spreading an appreciation and love of England among a class of readers brought up on the old anti-British historical tradition of their land, who were none the less becoming conscious of a turning of their hearts towards the old country. His book brought him many American friendships, and gave him an influence with leaders of opinion there. It put him into close personal and epistolary contact with Roosevelt, Cabot Lodge, Choate, the Adamses, John Hay, Elihu Root, the historians Rhodes and Van Tyne and many more. Van Tyne and other leaders of the historical movement in America that has recently criticised and revised the old ultra-patriotic tradition of the Revolution, had the highest admiration for my father's work. An incident that gave him particular pleasure was the presentation to him of a silver loving-cup with the following inscription :

To the Historian of the American Revolution from his friends —Theodore Roosevelt, Henry Cabot Lodge and Elihu Root.

In November 1904 Roosevelt wrote to him :

In my hours of leisure [during the Presidential campaign !] I did a good deal of reading. I re-read your history of our Revolution and liked it more than ever, but came to the conclusion that you had painted us a little too favourably. I also re-read both your Macaulay and your Fox, and then re-read Macaulay's History. It is a pretty good test of such a history to have a President who is also a candidate for the Presidency read it in the midst of a campaign.

My father's ' American Revolution,' a *magnum opus* of six volumes, begun when he was fifty-nine and finished when he was seventy-six, can hardly have the sustained excellence of the shorter works written in his prime, and the last volumes in particular show an exaggeration of his tricks of style and a curious inability to bring the work to a logical ending. Yet the vigour and artistry of the narrative is that of a master, though in a style less in fashion in the twentieth century than in the nineteenth. It was not so much that his powers had declined, as that his mind had ceased to move with the age. In 1876, when he brought out his uncle's Life, he was in the centre of the literary movement of the day ; but the ' American Revolution,' to English readers at least, was a voice from the past. The style of thinking and writing had great merit, but it was subtly out of fashion.

In saying this I would not underestimate either its considerable success in England or its still greater and more permanent success in America. The following letter of Henry James, written on the appearance of the second part in 1903, is the verdict of an artist, and incidentally describes the effect produced on transatlantic readers :

Rye, Sussex,
Nov. 25, 1903.

Dear Sir George,

I should be a poor creature if I had read your two last volumes without feeling the liveliest desire to write to you.

This new instalment of your admirable book has held
me so tight, from chapter to chapter, that it is as if I were
hanging back from mere force of appreciation, and yet I
found myself, as I read, vibrating responsively, in so many
different ways, that my emotions carried me at the same
time all over the place. You of course know far better
than I how you have dealt with your material ; but I
doubt whether you know what a work of civilization you
are perpetrating internationally by the very fact of your
producing so exquisite a work of art. The American,
the Englishman, the artist, and the critic in me—to say
nothing of the friend !—all drink you down in a deep
draught, each in turn feeling that he is more deeply concerned. But it is of course, as with the other volume, the
book's being so richly and authoritatively English, so
validly true, and yet so projected as it were into the
American consciousness, that will help to build the bridge
across the Atlantic.

It is this literary temperament of your work, this
beautiful quality of composition, and feeling of the presentation, grasping reality all the while, and controlling
and playing with the detail—it is this in our chattering
and slobbering day that gives me the sense of the ampler
tread and deeper voice of the man—in fact of his speaking
in his own voice at all, or moving with his own step. You
will make my own country people touch as with reverence
the hem of his garment ; but I think that I most envy you
your having such a method at all—your being able to see
so many facts and yet to see them each, imaged, and
related, and lighted as a painter sees the objects, together,
that are before his canvas. They become, I mean, so
amusingly concrete and individual for you ; but that is
just the unscrutable luxury of your book. And you bring
home, further, to me, at least, who had never so fully felt
it, what a difficult and precarious, and even might-not-
have-been, Revolution it was, altogether, as a Revolution.
Wasn't it as nearly as possible not being that ; whatever

else it might have been ?   The Tail might in time have taken to wagging the dog if the Tail could only, as seemed so easy, have been left on !   But I did not mean to embark on these reflections.   I only wanted really to make you feel a little responsible for my being, through living with you this succession of placid country evenings, far from the London ravage, extravagantly agitated.

But take your responsibility philosophically ; recall me to the kind consideration of Lady Trevelyan ; and

Believe me very constantly yours

HENRY JAMES.

Actually he never visited America.   He used to dwell with pride on the way he had got the correct atmosphere notwithstanding.   He was informed by some of his American friends that the only thing wrong in his local colouring was that he spoke of ' chapels,' whereas the places of worship were in fact spoken of as ' meeting-houses.'

Ever since his retirement from politics in 1897 he had been gradually withdrawing from society. In the first years of the new century he seldom appeared at the meetings of the Club, the Literary Society, Grillon's, or the Breakfast Club, where he had formerly been so much in his element.   And he had become a silent spectator of politics.   Until the war swallowed parties, he adhered in opinion to the Liberals, disapproving strongly the action of the House of Lords, admiring his old friends Campbell-Bannerman, Asquith and Grey, but finding neither the finance nor the oratory of twentieth-century Radicalism very much to his

SIR GEORGE TREVELYAN and THEODORE ROOSEVELT
at Welcombe.

taste. He was never tempted to intervene in the arena he had abandoned.

In 1911 he was included in the Order of Merit, an honour that he greatly appreciated. ' The whole thing is awfully enjoyable,' he wrote in boyish spirits and language to my wife, ' as enjoyable as the Gregory scholarship in 1856, and much more hardly earned.' He had been given everything for which he had any desire.

He kept his London house, 8, Grosvenor Crescent,[1] which had been his father's, but he latterly spent in it only two or three months of the year. In 1916 he sold it, and never came to London again.

His friendship with Theodore Roosevelt, that had arisen out of his ' American Revolution,' soon brought to light many other points of contact. They fairly delighted in one another, each having something the other had not but was well able to admire, and each being passionate readers of the same kind of history and literature. ' I have had a letter from Roosevelt,' he writes in November 1908, ' written in more tearing spirits than I thought the human bosom could contain.' Their friendship inspired a long correspondence, selections of which occupy the greater part of six chapters of Bishop's ' Life of Roosevelt,' including the long, amusing and most intimate narrative in which the ex-President described for my father's

[1] In the 'seventies and early 'eighties he had lived in 40 Ennismore Gardens, the end of a delightfully quiet *cul-de-sac* off Hyde Park.

benefit his celebrated tour of 1910 as the guest of
the crowned heads of old Europe, obsequious to
the great Republican, but unconscious of their
own approaching doom. When therefore the
catastrophe of 1914 overclouded the scene, it was
natural that the two friends should continue to
write to one another on public affairs in Europe
and America, with the perfect frankness that
had existed between them before the war. In
May 1915 my father wrote to Roosevelt from
Welcombe :

This morning I read the sentence in which you set forth
the *moral* side of the Munitions of War question—whether
they were to be employed for the rescue of Belgium, or for
her continued enslavement. The reading of it kindled
into a flame the smouldering consciousness which always
underlies my feelings—the consciousness that there is a
man in the world who is never wanting in chivalry,
humanity and the dictates of high national duty. You
know that you are my hero and always will be. . . . I
would pray ' God bless you ' in your great objects ; but
that word is of ill-omen to me. We had a noble battalion
of regular infantry quartered at Stratford-on-Avon. In
the course of six or seven weeks I became entirely at home
with them, officers and men alike ; and then they all
marched off to the war past our front gate, along the
Warwick road, with their baggage and Maxim guns,
bidding me good-by with jolly cries and assurances all
down the column. I bade the Colonel—a grand soldier
—' God bless you ' at the head of his regiment. Then the
news came. At the landing in the Dardanelles the
Colonel, the senior Major, and the Brigadier General were
killed at once ; and almost every marked young fellow in
that mess has gone to join them.

My father had disliked the brand of Imperialism that led to the Second Boer War. In January 1900 he had written to his sister Alice :

We have wasted our greatest national source of strength, the general conviction of the world that we can fight a great war if needful—on a quarrel which is not vital and which, in my opinion, might have been settled without fighting.

But his view of the Great War he thus expressed to a correspondent in November 1914 :

My personal view is that—after Austria had rejected Servia's reply to her ultimatum—Sir Edward Grey did his very utmost to avert war, and that he would have succeeded if Germany had frankly, sincerely, and promptly co-operated with him. Since then the situation was absolutely governed by the invasion of Belgium, and the enslavement or exile of the population. The independence, and the national existence, of the self-governing, industrial populations of Western Europe were thenceforward at stake. That is the opinion of all my many American friends, who are impartial and enlightened judges, and who have had the German case put before them with great energy by the Germans themselves. It is a burden which England cannot escape, and which, with due allowances made for human frailty and error, she has met in a way of which, as an Englishman, I am proud.

He regarded the war as the most unmitigated calamity and fully realised that it made an end of the civilisation to which he belonged. But he never thought that England could have kept out of it either with honour or with any likelihood of ultimate survival. Old age had come upon him,

L

and the most he could do for his country's cause was to keep up a voluminous correspondence on the war with many American friends of influence ranging from Roosevelt and Cabot Lodge downwards. Bryce, his friend of sixty years' standing, wrote to him throughout the war ' every ten days or a fortnight ; short letters, with something in every sentence and sending letters to read from his American correspondence.' The two held a kind of watching brief for the cause of Anglo-American relations.

When the war ended he was eighty years of age, feeble of body and no longer with the freshness of spirit to follow very closely the tragic convulsions of the sick and stricken world. The grey dawn of peace showed that the land-marks he knew had vanished in the night, and he was too old to join in the search for their successors. He lived in almost complete seclusion with my mother at Wallington and Welcombe, reading and dreaming of the past and awaiting in patience the too long lingering end.

His letters, like his talk and his daily thoughts, ran more and more on the past. This tendency, and a touch of old age in the style like the first frost on a flower, may be read in the following letter to his very old friend the Master of Trinity, written at Christmas 1917.

Dear Montagu Butler,
The year has brought round the day when for a long while past I have had the privilege and pleasure of writing to you, and reviewing the thoughts of so long, and such, a friendship. I doubt if a day ever passes without some-

LADY TREVELYAN
(Caroline Philips)

thing—and something connected with what is bright and never ignoble—reminds me of some event in our long connection, or in the shorter period when I knew you only as a distant, superhuman personage ; as for instance, when our whole family in the year 1848, including Macaulay, stood in front of the old Deanery at Peter-borough on the pretext of examining the tombstones ; which, more than half a century afterwards, the Bishop of Peterborough and I examined with great care, but found them obliterated by the weather ; so that the monument erected to a gentleman by his '*fiends*' was entirely illegible. The discovery of that inscription consoled Macaulay for the tedium of waiting in vain on the chance of a glimpse of you as you left the paternal home.[1]

During the last month I have read, most greedily and minutely, Monks's ' Life of Bentley.' No one can appre-ciate the book fully except a Trinity man, and especially *the* Trinity man who daily walks up and down the staircase [in the Master's Lodge] which was the *splendidissima causa* of the forty years' war between the great Master and his ill-starred senior fellows. I must frankly own that, against all principles of justice, my sympathies were increasingly with the terrible old prize-fighter, who in the end came out of the conflict triumphant. Frederic the Great in the Seven Years' War, and Bentley in his Forty Years' War, irresistibly command my sympathies. In both cases my uncle was too wise and firm to yield to that weakness. I am glad to know from many indications that the world, outside Germany, has come round to Macaulay's view of Frederic as against Carlyle's.

The last stage had now been reached. The form that extreme old age took with him was an

[1] Montagu Butler's father was Dean of Peterborough, 1842–53. My father, aged ten, had dragged his parents and uncle to the door to wait there on the chance of being able to show them young Montagu Butler, the god of his youthful idolatry !

undue shrinking from social intercourse, a fear of
having visitors in the house, though in fact when
they were there he talked to them with his old
eagerness, enjoyment and brilliancy, and sent
them away fascinated and rejoicing at their
reception.

The very perfection of his domestic happiness
with my mother and his library drew him away
from the world ; it was a gradual process, extended
over thirty years, and it finally became only too
complete, though society and friendship were
always open to him in such abundance whenever
he chose. His kinsman, Sydney Holland, the
second Lord Knutsford, whose breezy utterances
were always full of real meaning, wrote to me
after his death :

It always struck me that your father was an intensely
shy man.   Everyone I ever met who knew him said what
a brilliant conversationalist he was, and every time I met
him that was the impression left.   His leaving the world
and retiring into solitude was rather an instance of what
I mean about his shyness.   No man could have had more
close friends if he had desired them.

There is a measure of truth in this—though he
had close friends, he might easily have enlarged
their number. No doubt he was, on one side, a
shy man, though it may seem an odd word to use
of one who was a great social success whenever he
chose to live in London, and who on all occasions
so readily kept the conversational ball on the
move. But his mind was sufficient for itself, it
worked by its own processes, and as he grew

old he became impatient if they were often
interrupted.

He had his own emotional, historical and
literary way of looking at the world and all that
happened in it. A piece of news, domestic or
public, was never a mere fact to him ; if it
interested him at all, he must needs find a place
for it in his artistic-emotional scheme of things ;
he must compare it to one of the humorous or
hallowed happenings of history, set it in some ideal
or literary light. This habit of mind always
coloured, though it sometimes blurred, his vision.
His common talk was never commonplace.
Everything was endued by him with a certain
glamour, if it was to be noticed at all. It followed
that he sometimes gave to things or persons
imaginary qualities that they had not. He was
only half at home with the world except when he
had subdued it to his medium. His talk was not
stilted—it was often jocular and homely—but it
always flowed in an artificial form of his own
creating. It was perfectly natural to him because
it represented the real texture of his mind, and it
was the secret of his success as an orator, as a
talker and as a writer. His clear and beautiful
voice and the courtesy of his demeanour added to
the charm of his conversation.

He was specially fond of two young men,
Geoffrey and Hilton Young, the sons of his old
friend Sir George. The continuance into another
generation of the old family friendship appealed
strongly to his imagination, and he found in both

their personalities that spark and distinction that he sought for in everything. After his death Geoffrey Young wrote to me :

What was it that made him unique, in one's memories, that gave him a quality of rarity that no other possessed, so that his momentary interest in what you had to say seemed a compliment which left a long after-glow ; and his exquisite personal concern in oneself for oneself, when it came, went right through one, something sacred in memory for its impersonal beauty ? Of course, the amazing intellectual brilliance, refined and refined again until it was crystalline in its clarity. With this the tremendous vitality of interest, curiosity, enthusiasm, until an impersonal standard of the ' best ' seemed to be established, and that everything—things of the mind, of the body, of art, of comfort, of the ridiculous. And then, with that as an ' absolute,' the human show might go past, in all its confusion, and the passing flower of its beauty, the very crest of the wave of happenings, the cream of its best absurdities, would be caught and enjoyed—just the best and that only, and for the instant of its freshness and sparkle.

Of course that was formidable. I shall never forget the sort of delirious and amused terror with which, in my talks as a young man, I waited for the inevitable second when the light would go out in the extraordinary eyes, the voice would become courteous and uninterested, and he would turn away, on a sentence that clearly was not interesting enough to himself to finish ! And yet one could never feel the least injured. It was so obviously and entirely impersonal. The interest was gone from the point or the subject, the crest of the wave was past, for you as for him. Another might come, even as he turned away, and in a flash you were drawn into it again with him.

Formidable and delightful, and one loved it, because the standard was so personally unconscious and high. It

SIR GEORGE TREVELYAN

In his study at Wallington.

wouldn't however have meant so much if it had only been
an intellectual rarity. What made it great was the equal
and greater value attached to all other human qualities
judged by the same high and perfected standard. That
splendid simplicity of admiration for qualities of
character, not only of the mind ! And a simplicity
intellectually achieved, based upon such experience of,
experiments with, human nature :—an ironic, almost a
cynical understanding. A talk in his study after the
return from the war stays with me a memory apart. It
was only a gesture or two and a few sentences. But it
was enough to change the value, for me, of certain human
qualities, glimpsed for a second in the atmosphere of an
undertaking like his. It was greatness of heart that made
him great.

This I believe is true, and touches on the
essential reason why he was of note as a writer and
as a man. But though his heart was great, his
vision and sympathy were limited. He might so
easily have had many more friends, as Knutsford
said—he might have taken interest in so many
more things, as Henry Sidgwick once complained
to me. But then would this quality of his have
remained of the same lustre? I cannot tell. It
is hard to say when and how far the limitations
of a man's qualities are essential conditions of
those qualities. At any rate his mind was
selective, wilfully so sometimes, yet working
perhaps on some half-conscious principle of self-
knowledge.

The likeness of his mind to Macaulay's is
obvious ; the one was moulded on the other.
But the two men were very different. My father

was refined, with a complex refinement half of the old English upper class, and half of the artist of all countries and ages. His uncle had neither of these kinds of refinement : he was of the middle class, knowing by rub of shoulders the world through which he had forced his way up so quickly in his youth. Though an artist in achievement, Macaulay was no more an artist in temperament than Sir Walter Scott himself. One of the things my father said to me in his last hours I had never heard him say before. He was, of course, talking of 'uncle Tom,' in the broken accents of the dying. He was 'a common man,' he said, repeating it several times. Needless to say the phrase was used in no derogatory sense. And indeed Macaulay was 'the man in the street,' but with genius, scholarship, statesmanship and encyclopædic knowledge added. My father, with a smaller measure of those gifts, was in his innermost nature an aristocrat and an artist. Partly for that reason intellectuals like John Morley, who were jealously indignant at Macaulay's great fame, warmed to the nephew who worshipped him.

At the beginning of 1928 my father and mother had been married for nearly sixty years, and had spent very few days apart. It seemed neither likely nor desirable that one would long survive the other. In January my mother died at Welcombe, and was buried at Snitterfield hard by, in a plot of land that she had given to her

WALLINGTON

neighbours as a graveyard. The inscription on her tomb, which my father just survived to approve, recalls her as :

By nature courteous and gentle towards all, and full of tender concern for the welfare of others. A skilful painter of the landscapes she loved so well. Above all singularly blest in almost sixty years of happy married life.

In May my father was just able to bear the journey from Warwickshire to his Northumbrian home, where he desired to die. He lingered there for three months. It gave him a faint glow of pleasure that he turned ninety at the end of July, winning that last race by a head. Beyond that he had no wish to stay. He died at Wallington on August 16, 1928, and was buried amid a concourse of his Northumbrian neighbours on the hill top in Cambo churchyard, under the church tower which his father had raised. It stands, a far-seen landmark overlooking the countryside that they had both loved so well, with its woodlands, its stone farms, its great grass fields and more distant heather moors, from Shafto crags in the south to Simonside bounding the northern horizon.

EXCERPTS FROM LETTERS

SOME EXCERPTS FROM LETTERS OF SIR GEORGE TREVELYAN TO HIS SON ROBERT

THE following samples from my father's correspondence on literary and general topics, occurring in ordinary domestic letters of business and affection, will serve, I hope, to supplement the impression I have tried to convey in the Memoir.

Nov. 4, 1891. Rome. Dear Bob.—We spent this morning in Pompeii, that is to say we went back 1800 years for a couple of hours. It is a most wonderful illusion. You go in at the city gate, under a large, low arch through which the carriage-way runs, while a smaller arch takes in the foot passengers, and in a moment you are in classical times. The pavement of the streets, and the high paths on both sides, are exactly what they were ; and, though the houses are unroofed, still they are so utterly unlike modern houses that the illusion is complete. It is like a town that children make with bricks—a forum, and theatre, and baths, and taverns, and any amount of gentleman's houses ; all perfectly clean, and neat and finished. There is an indescribable sense of its being an entirely different society from that in which we live, and there is nothing in the least incongruous with what we know of Roman times. You feel that Martial and Horace might have lived there, just as Rudyard Kipling might be written by people who lived in Anglo-Indian society and houses.

Dec. 9, 1891. Wallington. I hope you will go into the examination determined to *enjoy* it ; to do it in a *scientific* manner, without troubling yourself about the result : but determined only that, when it is over, you shall feel that you have done the very utmost with the means at your disposal. Above all remember that, till it is over, it is your duty to put everything except the examination out of your head.

Nov. 29, 1902. Wallington. I envy Bessie her first visit to Paris. Mine was at fifteen years of age, when all the houses were new built, and the uniforms varied and brilliant, and the military bands banging about the Rue de Rivoli, and gilt on the rails of the Tuileries garden, and on the gingerbread generally. [1853.]

June 16, 1903. Welcombe. I have just read Theocritus down to the end of the Gorgo and Praxinoe, writing the words I did not know in pencil, so as to avoid the trouble of looking them out another time. I looked out as many as 36 in a single Idyl ; and yet there was nothing in all the fifteen or sixteen poems (for poems indeed they are) which I could not perfectly understand. He is a most forcible and original writer ; and, if you do not know a word, and have to look it out, it often turns out to be something very far from what you expect, and yet quite appropriate and effective. I finished to-day the *De Senectute* with great delight ; and shall re-read the *De Amicitia* and after awhile the *De Officiis.* That sort of thing tunes one's mind for one's morning's work. Give my best love to Elizabeth. I am glad she is reading ' Clarissa.' There is no skipping in it : but after a time the thing catches hold of you, and you care for nothing else. I regard her short letter to Lovelace as, in its way, the most extraordinary thing in literature—certainly the greatest surprise, when the meaning flashes over you, as it did over him.

Nov. 5, 1903. Wallington. [Another part of his
' American Revolution ' just coming out.]   It is after the
first fortnight, when the first lot of readers have finished
or broken down in a book, that its fate is settled.   We
have had a famous old Harrovian shooting party—Ridley,
Belper, Kenelm Digby, Charles and I.   They all shot well,
and Ridley splendidly.   It is delightful meeting old friends,
and increasing old friendships which had been loosened by
politics for so long a time.   [Lord] Belper is great fun ;
a humourist of a rough and strong sort, and a most
wonderful man of public business ; but *au fond* the same
as ever.   He took up an old argument about whether I
ought to have lent him a gun-bag on a rainy day in Ireland
at exactly the point at which it was left 41 years ago.

Feb. 3, 1904. Welcombe.   I have just finished the
Satires, Epistles and Ars Poetica of Horace.   I was surprised to find how little I knew of the Ars, and was much
impressed with its great inferiority as poetry, and the
excellence of it as a *treatise* on literary performance ;
though its precepts would rather teach to write prose than
poetry.   His inspiration seems to have died out in the
interval between the Epistle to Julius Florus, which is a
golden poem, and the Ars ; but his common sense and
insight remained.   I should say that it was a theme
suggested from a high quarter, like the Georgics, and
that he died before revising and emending it.

April 2, 1904. Welcombe.   I am easing off work [at
the ' American Revolution '], and, after finishing
' Lucretius,' have begun on Bergk's ' Poetæ Græci,' and
intend reading it through.   It is the perfection of poetry,
in a society exactly suited to it.   I have the old letter you
wrote about it, in which you say that Verrall has proved
that Tyrtaeus dates from ' the sixth century.'   I suppose
that means that he was touched up or written [written
down as distinct from repeated or sung] in the 6th century

B.C. The Messenian war was in the 7th century B.C.
The fragments of Tyrtoeus were taken from Aristotle,
Diodorus, Plutarch, Pausanias and Strabo.

June 22, 1904. Dijon. We had a most interesting
evening at Geneva. I always think that the *most* wonderful combination of young genius, at its best, without an
atom of pretension, was when Byron had left England in
his great trouble, and when Shelley, Mary Godwin, and
Claire were living close to him on the Lake of Geneva.
There are some exquisitely humorous letters of Byron's
and Hobhouse's, relating how the English in Geneva
looked through telescopes at the Villa Diodati and reported
home that there were ladies ' on the balcony.' We dis-
covered the Villa Diodati, whose occupants were absent,
and the woman in charge showed us all over it—the same,
exactly the same, as it was in Byron's day when he wrote
there the 3rd canto of ' Childe Harold.' There was a
glorious old balcony, in wrought iron, with the Diodati
arms, running round three sides of the house above the
terrace. Then, three or four hundred yards below, across
the vineyards, was Shelley's house, which I examined well
from the outside. Mama has sketched them both. It
was as interesting as Keats's and the Brawnes' villa
at Hampstead, and as authentic ; but far, far more
beautiful.

May 25, 1905. Grosvenor Crescent. The review in
The Times of Brandes was very good. The writer has a
great, manly, and, to my mind, almost unerring judgement
of poetry. I think it was he who said that Wordsworth
might have been a parson, or Shelley an agitator, but that
Keats could not have been anything but a poet. I rather
take, more than most people, the continental view of
Byron. If I want to find a specimen of much that is best
in the old Greek, Aristophanes, the Greek lyrics and
elegiacs, the best Lucan, Juvenal, etc., I find it in Byron,

besides much that is of course of a more offhand and even sloppy sort.

July 20, 1905. Wallington. Mind you read the composite autobiography of Gibbon—the one that held the market for a century and a quarter, put together by Miss Holroyd. It is six times better than the six genuine ones. I almost wish they had never been unearthed.

Dec. 6, 1905. Palace Hotel, Rome. We are settled in the most ideal place :—on the fifth floor of a beautiful new hotel, overlooking Rome just across the centre, not seeing the Vatican on the one side or the Capitol and Palatine on the other. In fact we see the Campus Martius, and the Rome of Sixtus the Fifth and Leo the Tenth. Then we have a glorious view across the Tiber of the Acqua Paola and Garibaldi's statue, seeing all that slope nearly from end to end.

' Hinc septem dominos videre montes
Et totam licet æstimare Romam.

That is true of St. Pietro in Montorio but not of us, but I am well contented with our view. We are rather living a Roman life than sight-seeing with any perceptible effort, and it is very enjoyable. I am reading the *De Naturâ Deorum*, having finished the end of the Tusculan Disputations and the first five books of Martial. The place is pretty full of Americans. The humbler Americans, of whom three-fourths at least are women, are a very decent set of people who take great interest in the place according to their lights. On Thanksgiving Day we dined at their Embassy on roast turkey and cranberry sauce. It is a great thing for Mama to have some freedom from occupation, and be able to sketch and enjoy herself.

Jan. 29, 1906. Welcombe. Thanks for your jolly letter. These are indeed great times. [The sweeping

Liberal victory at the elections after twenty years of party eclipse.] George has just come here from Acland's Richmond election. The poll was declared in that beautiful hill-town, which Turner so often painted. It happens that I am just reading Catullus through, without notes, but with a classical dictionary ; and for the first time I have fully realised that he was a Roman aristocrat of the great time : the lover of Clodius's sister ; the personal enemy and disparager of Cæsar's party. The people whom he chaffs and satirises, or whose epithalamiums he writes, were not the middle-class rag-tag and bobtail of Martial and Juvenal, but men who had histories —most of them tragical ones—in the coming years.

Sept. 23, 1906. Wallington. I have looked through three volumes of the Yellow Book, which exactly answers to your recollection. There is observable in it a certain *collective* energy and enthusiasm, which makes everybody do more vigorously, or at any rate more oddly, what they regard as their ideal. James's two stories are very strong. Sickert's things are most curious—in a way better than Beardsley's. We have the Charles Adamses here—a pleasant couple. He is going on to Flodden, with great enthusiasm, which is well for 71. His great grandfather was deeply interested in the world up to 90. Adams has seen even bigger battles than Flodden. He was asleep in his saddle during Pickett's charge at Gettysburg.

Nov. 21, 1906. Wallington. I read Keats's unrhymed sonnet three or four times. The letter to Reynolds containing it is, as you say, a charming effusion. What a delightful genius ! The very passages in a less attractive vein—like that beginning ' I'll cavern you, and grotto you ' in the letter of March 1818—increase one's feeling of his native refinement and elevation, by showing the *milieu* from which he came.

Dec. 12, 1909. Welcombe. It is very interesting about the *Wasps* [Greek Play at Cambridge]. You know my strong views about the Parabases of Aristophanes—that they were sung or spoken as clearly and intelligibly as Grossmith's patter. The extreme literary excellence and finish—greater than that of the Iambics—seems to prove that.

Feb. 26, 1910. Welcombe. Your letter, received this morning, was very welcome. We are much interested about the name [of his new grandchild]. I shall be greatly gratified if Otto is the second name. As to the first, Julian is very nice, especially as Elizabeth has a liking for it. The connection of ' John ' with our family is perhaps unexampled in England. In 170 years, between Henry VI and Charles I, *eight* John Trevelyans succeeded each other, father and son, at Nettlecombe ; stout, solid fellows, I make no doubt, who could keep goods and gear together. Then came two Georges, and two very long-lived and not insignificant Johns.

Sept. 9, 1910. Wallington. As to Clough, I have long thought the ' Amours de Voyage ' the best of all his works, as a whole, and have read it often, aloud and to myself. Whatever it is worth, nothing can be more finished : and the little pieces of verse, at the beginning and end of the books, are in a delicious vein. [My father's first present to my mother had been Clough's poems.]

April 19, 1912. Grosvenor Crescent. I am glad that you approved Arnold Bennett's play, and expect to find it just what you say. If for no other reason, I am really curious to see what so very remarkable a writer will make of the drama. Yesterday I spent some while writing letters to replace what have probably gone down in the *Titanic*. I earnestly hope it may put a stop to the idle, vulgar, foolish luxury of travel. Louis Seize rooms, and

Louis Quinze rooms at £800 a suite : a squash racket-court, and enormous banquets every day, rough or fine. The essence of a ship is to be well-found, neat and scrupulously clean. I suppose vulgar people go in their hundreds to sea, as they travel on land, to get a sort of luxury which they cannot afford at home. They have spoiled all real goodness in hotels : and they have now spoiled ship life, which had a charm of its own.

June 3, 1912. Welcombe. I have been reading Lady Shelley's diary—*not* Mary Godwin's family, but another. It contains by far the pleasantest, and, I doubt not, truest, picture of Wellington at the height of his career that has ever been given to the world. We are reading Ruskin aloud. I cannot account for more not having been said in praise of Cook's life of him, except that Ruskin's inordinate mass of writing, and his extraordinary want of self-control, and his ravings about myths and etymologies, tire the ordinary reader more than we are aware.

Oct. 21, 1913. Wallington. I am rather proud of going to Rome when I am older than even St. Peter when he went—or did not go. I always thought the details of Italian scenery so much less attractive than English, and often so *queer* : but the manner in which the masses *compose* is wonderful. What is there like the opposite bank and background from the North bank of the Arno at Florence ?

Jan. 23, 1915. Welcombe. We have a battalion of regular infantry quartered in the town [Stratford], fresh from India, who are sent to these pleasant quarters to 'acclimatize' before going to the front. They use the park [at Welcombe] for drill, and we see a good deal, very pleasantly, of the officers. The change between the army of my youth, and the army now, is extraordinary. The men are really most respectable and good fellows ;

M

and the officers are exceedingly hard-working and homely, without any side or pretension whatever. The wives, who show the tone unconsciously, are very nice, quiet, cheerful and contented women, under trying circumstances of a career. I have just read from the 21st to the 35th of Livy, with great and increasing admiration. All the details of serious Roman life never get into the English histories.

April 9, 1915. Welcombe. [Written when suffering from a disabled arm.] I have thought pretty often about Lord Nelson lately, and especially at breakfast-time. I wonder often how he managed to eat a boiled egg. Perhaps Lady Hamilton helped him.

Dec. 15, 1915. Welcombe. We are much interested in your statistics of the Library : you got a wonderful lot for the money, though it reads large in francs. Do you remember the private tutor at Geneva in the eighteenth century writing to the London banker that his son had got into debt ' 10,000 *livres* ' ; and how the banker drove straight off to Geneva, and how, when he learned the state of the case, he merely said, ' Oh ! seulement ces petites choses là,' and drove straight back to London.

July 20, 1916. Wallington. I am glad the dear boy learns by heart what he likes, and learns it well. I have the strongest feeling about a child, and a youth, never learning by heart *quantity*, but *quality*. I absolutely ruined what I suppose is a good memory, by always having to learn about twice as much, and in the case of our sixth form Monday morning lesson at least six times as much as I could learn accurately. I have distinctly improved myself of late years by learning a few pieces otherwise. To-day I became 78 years old, and I finished Thucydides. I began it on the 20th

January, and read it off and on about 100 mornings.
The 8th book is about half of it less interesting : but I
agree with Jackson that the account of the scoundrelly
plot of Pisander, and the Whig counter-revolution of
Theramenes, is equal to most things in history.

June 11, 1917. Welcombe. I quite agree in your
analysis of what is to me hopelessly arid in Swinburne,
that his processes of intellect were ' at their best '
curiously ' unconscious and automatic,' and ' at their
worst mechanical.' Nothing to me is more barren and
devoid of real knowledge, than his political poems.
Compare them with the end of Browning's *Old
Pictures at Florence*, with the scene of the Naples
coast, ' touched in the liver wing,' etc. ; or with the
conversation of Luigi and his mother in *Pippa Passes !*
His gross and violent ignorance of that singular, many-
sided, visionary Louis Napoleon is absurd in one who
makes him the main person in his repertory. It is as
if a schoolboy said to himself ' Here's a tyrant. I will
write, what one writes about tyrants, at least once a
year while he lives, and when he goes to eternal fire
(which I do not believe in) I will set my mark on him
to all futurity.'

Aug. 4, 1917. Wallington. Runciman drove over his
wife in a little motor, with Edward Grey, and they spent
the day with us. Grey is tranquil and not unhappy in
his retirement. What trials he has had ! The violent
deaths of such a wife and such a brother ; the terrible
inroad on his health ; his impaired eyesight ; and the
utter destruction by fire of his house, which he so deeply
loved. Late in life he is most eager about books.

Aug. 20, 1917. Wallington. The times are strange,
and perhaps the strangest proof of it is the oversetting
of very familiar British institutions. To-day is the first

day of black-game shooting ; and we have been eating
grouse and black-game for exactly a fortnight, at a lunch
which begins at 12.30 !

Oct. 5, 1917. Wallington.   Here we see a succession
of young men from the front, who impress me very
favourably.   There must be a very real consideration shown towards them.   There are two brothers
Herdman ;   one a Canadian immigrant who used to
work in our garden, and the other an English lad.
They never see anything of each other in their distant
quarters of that vast front ;   but their officers arranged
for them having their home leave together last Christmas.
This month their mother had a very dangerous operation ;   and the Englishman begged that the Canadian
brother might be sent home to see her through it, because
he was ' her favourite son,' and the whole thing was
arranged most promptly and kindly.   I am reading in
Livy how the Romans began to have military pay, and
to serve in winter at the siege of Veii.

1918.   We have a changed Wallington, with the great
pastures to the North all turned into arable land, and
the woods reverting to their pristine wildness.

April 19, 1918. Welcombe.   I really like getting the
War documents from Trinity which come to me as (I
suppose) the oldest Fellow of the College.   By the way
I cannot remember whether I sent you the most interesting and pleasant letter which Sir Joseph Thomson
wrote me.   It was very satisfactory as showing what a
frank, kindly man he is, and then how very much of a
scholar, besides being a man of science of the very highest
rank.   It was an excellent appointment.   He writes in
eager appreciation of Monk's Bentley, in language that
shows he was a true scholar.

Dec. 1, 1918. Welcombe. The biggest thing, by far, in history has happened. The three great autocratic empires, which constitute two-thirds of Europe and half of Asia, are in absolute dissolution. George used to say that the effect of universal service in those despotic countries was that in Austria, Germany, and Russia political freedom and national aspirations were entirely hopeless, because all the able-bodied citizens were enrolled under arms. So it was, and I anticipated that it would always be so ; but it now turns out that, when discontent and disaster reach a certain point, the revolution comes like Noah's flood, and leaves no land visible above the water. Three hundred millions of people are now in such a wild state of confusion that no one can anticipate what will happen, or even understand what is happening.

May 21, 1919. Welcombe. Uncle Tom changed his view of Euripides at five and thirty years old : but I have taken till near 81 to know what Euripides is at his best. I have yesterday finished the Bacchæ, and agree with Gilbert Murray that ' for excitement, for mere thrill, there is absolutely nothing like it in ancient literature.' The sustaining of such a theme, at such a level, is nothing less than superhuman. Apparently, after verse 1340, Agave spoke a famous dirge which is lost to us ; and there the play should have ended : and what a play it would have been ! Up to that line it is faultless.

A few excerpts may be of interest from letters which my father wrote in old age to his daughter-in-law, Mrs. Robert Trevelyan.

May 26, 1910. Welcombe. Dear Elizabeth.—Pray thank Robert for his letter which interested us much. We too are sorely *excédés* by the King's death, as treated by the newspapers. The *real* emotions and sentiments about this sort of event—and with me they have been genuine—are so overlaid and vulgarised by the perfunctory gush of writers who do not care about the matter at all. The very comet has been made ridiculous, and a humbug. I have seen two dozen columns about it; and no newspapers that I have seen have told the cardinal fact that it has been increasing in remoteness, and coming down in size, ever since it was a terror to the Turks in 1456.

Aug. 19, 1910. Wallington. I got out to Ray [Sir Charles Parsons' Northumbrian estate] and had a long day, from 10 to 7, grouse driving, and enjoyed it greatly. There was a bright blue sky, with white fleecy clouds in the shapes of animals, all over it: which seen from those heights was glorious. I got 10 or 11 brace myself and am always glad to be with those excellent neighbours. Mrs. Sidgwick has just gone. She was quietly happy and cheerful and seemed very glad to be with us.

July 30, 1911. Wallington. I went out this morning, a delicious morning after rain, and inside the portico was a little girl, in a sort of ecstasy of happiness, singing and talking to a kitten which she held in her arms. Carry tells me that it must have been May Entiknap. I am glad they are here and so agreeably lodged. It is a very attractive way of doing one's politics, reading the letters in *Times* from all and sundry, at Wallington. I suppose that it will all be over on Friday. [Passage of Parliament Act.] Certainly the unexpected has played a great part as it always does in a revolution.

Jan. 30, 1912. I was greatly interested by your having the 'Cossacks.' Very many years ago, before the ordinary Englishman had ever heard of Tolstoi, I read it in a yellow-backed English translation, I almost think without the name of the author, and thought it wonderfully romantic and charming. I have since read it several times in French ; but I have read still oftener the three wonderful pieces that are usually bound up with it, the scenes from the Siege of Sebastopol. They are his personal experiences, the raw material of the wonderful battle-pieces in ' La Guerre et la Paix.' They are the best account of war ever written, and that ever will be written : the best that ever Tolstoi wrote in any department ; and you know what that means.

Sep. 20, 1918. Wallington. We are thinking a great deal about you and Julian. It is curious (considering how utterly I forget almost every detail of my then life) that I have the clearest recollection of my father's taking me to school in Hertfordshire the 5th of this same month, seventy-two years ago—a little boy just turned eight. It struck me much that he, popularly believed and probably rightly to be the busiest man in England, should have given up a whole day for the purpose.

Dec. 25, 1923. Mamma this morning received a delightful Christmas letter from Robert. It warmed our hearts, on a morning when the glass had fallen 15 degrees in the 24 hours. We were interested to hear of Julian's happy industries over his drawings and painting. I greatly liked his black and white drawing for Aunt Anna, and his bold, cheerful landscape which he sent to Mamma. I think his and Pauline's artistic handiness comes through Mamma ; for I am as absolutely without it (having tried it eagerly and laboriously when young) as I am without an ear for music, or any rudimentary conception of mathematics, as distinct from arithmetic, or any linguistic faculty at all.[1] All these four things

---

[1] His French accent was very bad, and he knew no other foreign modern language. But the amount of Greek, Latin and French which he read for pleasure was much greater than the amount read by ninety-nine well educated people out of a hundred.

are accomplishments, which heaven gives or denies. You
have your full share of them.

The following letter, written to Lord Rosebery
in April 1922, recalls a social institution of a
bygone age, famous in its day, the Breakfast Club :

Dear Rosebery, As the Greeks said, ἱππέας εἰς τὸ
πεδίον καλεῖς by asking me to write about the Breakfast Club. I entirely agree with you about having
guests to breakfast and about breakfasting out. But I
am glad to explain to you *why* the Breakfast Club had
exceptional attractions about it. It met on Saturday,
once a fortnight, during the Session of Parliament ; and
practically that came to about ten meetings in the
London Season. And we met, not at an hotel or
restaurant, but at our own houses ; and the household
all took pride in doing it well, and soon had traditions
of service and cuisine. But the great feature of it was
that the members were *real friends*, who looked forward
to meeting each other, and made a duty and certainty
of attending, like the members of Johnson's Club in the
ten earliest and all-famous years. As to friendship, I
will name to you the active members of the Club during
my central period. Nominally there were twelve ; but
some of them were always abroad on high service—
Dufferin for instance and Lansdowne. Those whom I
was sure of meeting were Wolseley, Reay, Sir Alfred
Lyall, Herschell, Courtenay, Goschen, Ilbert and
Mackenzie Wallace. Grant Duff was there too, greatly
respected, silent and rather sad ; for he was old at
seventy-five ; most prematurely so, as it seems to me
who have reached about the age of Sir Henry Holland,
or (for the matter of that) Benjamin Franklin. Like the
' Apostles ' at Cambridge there were nominally twelve,
and really eight or nine ; and one looked forward to
being in a circle of true and congenial friends. Of

course the sacrifice of Saturday morning was a serious matter. Lubbock and (I believe) John Morley would not join the Club for that reason. But it was the holiday in the week; and we had earned it and enjoyed it. *One* guest might be asked by the host, and he had to be a foreigner. The most successful, and to me deeply interesting, guest whom I remember was Baron Hübner, who was apostrophized by Louis Napoleon on New Year's Day, 1859 [1] and who wrote *Une année de ma vie.* He had been the subject of the Latin epigram by which I got the medal at Cambridge as a lad in 1859, which was the best piece of Latin I ever wrote. He breakfasted at my house, with the Club, in 1890 or 1891, when he was over eighty, but so young and so infinitely pleasant. The Club was given up in 1911, after Lyall's death. That was a signal which was wisely taken.

The following are excerpts from letters of my father to his elder sister Margaret, wife of Sir Henry Holland, later Lord Knutsford :

Oct. 29, 1881. Castellamare. Dear Margaret, I have thought of you very much the last few days, as the person who would enter into my feelings about them. Rome, strange to say, seemed to me full of my uncle. When I sate in the forum alone, repeating his lines, I found myself crying sadly and bitterly ; not over Caesar and Cicero, heaven knows, but at the thought of the poorness and slightness of the men, who are great men now, as compared with his strong and noble simplicity. And in St. Peter's I seemed to realise him in a way I never did before. The amount of time he spent there, the frequency with which he returned there, show a power of being amused which I never realised before. The result was that I

---

[1] Hübner was Austrian Ambassador in France. The carefully prepared words that Napoleon publicly said to him on that famous occasion gave the world its first warning of the coming Franco-Austrian war in Italy.

resolved to ask you to let Carry bring back the journal of his 1838 tour, that I may read it at leisure in these winter evenings.

Sep. 3, 1882. Chief Secretary's Lodge. Ireland. [End of the police strike in Dublin.] Yesterday was the critical day ; and things then took the right turn, instead of the wrong. All the men, who were wavering, have gone on duty in an excellent spirit ; and the men who were dismissed are unhappy and repentant. The forces of disorder and disaffection, which are always on the watch, have been checkmated. Of course it would be most unwise to be prematurely confident in so great a business : for this has really been the revolutionary spirit, which has run riot in Ireland for the last four years, producing its effect on the constabulary. But I am quite satisfied that our action was the right action ; that it was executed successfully in detail ; and the results have been better than I ventured to hope for it. The military have been in our house for the last forty hours. They have just been withdrawn and we have again our old guard of Dublin police and constabulary, to our mutual satisfaction.

Dec. 20, 1883. Chief Secretary's Lodge. I every day read Carlyle's Frederic, and have now got down to Frederic William's death, with great interest and edification. I never could get through that part of it before. Last year I read the last half of Carlyle's Cromwell, which I never could finish before, with deep interest. The fact is that it is not literature, but life of a high and arduous sort, portrayed with miraculous knowledge of the relation of that sort of life to human nature ; and it is only when you have a great burden on you that you even understand it, and then it is wonderfully suggestive and inspiring.

Oct. 16, 1896. Wallington. I feel the Archbishop's [Benson's] death very deeply. I am almost ashamed to say how fond I was of him personally. I love a clergyman who treats me as a real friend and equal, and at the same time is a real clergyman, not affecting, in off moments, the man of the world. How striking what you say about Gladstone ! You remember that he was at Lord Granville's when the Bishop of Winchester was killed on his ride thither from the station. Henry Cowper was there, and said that he never appreciated before what an immense blessing it was to be an orator. Lord Granville, he said, was silent and depressed all the evening and Gladstone too, till he pronounced him ' a great Diocesan,' after which the phrase pleased him so much that he was greatly consoled. It answers to his saying of poor Benson ' He died like a soldier ' !

Poor Harry [Lord Knutsford] to have finished Hogg ! [Life of Shelley.] If he would read the two volume Life of Mrs. Shelley, and Dowden's Shelley, and then Kegan Paul's Life of Godwin, he will prolong the delight indefinitely. I would gladly read them all again.

Dec. 29, 1896. Wallington. I have been reading aloud *Shirley*. One finds it very inferior to the other two, but good. To-day we read the schoolfeast of the three parishes. The book says that there were twenty tables, each for twenty guests : and at the end of the chapter comes one of our dear Mamma's sums, that uncle Tom used to laugh at her about :

$$
\begin{array}{r}
20 \\
20 \\
\hline
400
\end{array}
$$

July 4, 1903. Wallington. I am giving myself a complete holiday, reading Cicero and Theocritus, and the new volume of de Gorce's History of the Second Empire. It is the account of Hohenzollern candidature. I know few things more interesting than a good account, written with full knowledge, of the great events of one's own life time. It is like living it through again ; only that you see the inner reality of things, and not the outward appearance of them. I am inclined to think that Bismarck did not *make* the incident in order to bring on a war, but that he *used* it, when the French gave themselves away, and rushed into a trap which the Powers above had set.

Sept. 29, 1903. Wallington. This is our wedding day —34 years ago. We began life with three maid servants ; and two of them are in the house at this moment. Happy years they have been ; and fortunate, beyond all deserts, has been my lot. We hope that Charles will settle in the village here, like Charles Musgrove [in *Persuasion*]. Carry will not accuse Mary's nursemaid of gadding ; and Mary, when they dine with us, shall have due precedence as the grand-daughter of a baronet.

May 28, 1904. Wallington. I have taken a holiday to-day ; and, whenever I do, I feel like the heroine in *Pippa passes*. What a poem it is ! So full of beauty, humour, knowledge of Italy, and knowledge of mankind. There is nothing, so far as I know, which is at once so perfect, and so unlike anything else in the world. I have spent my morning reading Greek, and read more than three hundred lines of Theognis,—old Greek poetry near 600 years before Christ—without any notes and with delight. I would not have done that in old days. There is an extraordinary interest about the Greek poetry of the Aegean sea and Asia Minor, long before Athenian days. It was *the* time for Greek poetry ; a very joyous, keen, and, in some ways, highly civilised life. The Athenians seem to have had no poets except their dramatists.

HORACE AT THE UNIVERSITY OF ATHENS

THIS little extravaganza is at the disadvantage of having been composed for acting, and altered for printing. It lays claim, however, to perfect historical accuracy, as it faithfully records the known occurrences in the life of Horace ; his residence at Athens as a student ; his enlistment in the republican army ; his behaviour at Philippi ; his pardon at the instance of Mæcenas ; and his appointment to a post in the Roman Treasury. That it is accepted by undergraduates as a fair representation of undergraduate life and thought is testified by the local demand having brought it through three editions. The passages that refer to the fighting then taking place in Virginia will serve as specimens of the tone in which young Englishmen of the day wrote and talked about the greatest event of our time. [Author's note to earlier editions.]

DRAMATIS PERSONÆ

AUGUSTUS.
MÆCENAS.
BRUTUS.
CASSIUS.
CAIUS,
BALBUS,
HORACE,   *Students of the University*
DECIUS MUS,   *of Athens.*
SEMPRONIUS VIRIDIS, *a Freshman,*
THE VICE-CHANCELLOR OF THE UNIVERSITY.
THE PUBLIC ORATOR.
QUINTUS RUSSELLUS MAXIMUS, *the Special Correspondent of the* ' Acta Diurna.'
THE GHOST OF CÆSAR.
LYDIA.
STUDENTS, SOLDIERS, GUARDS, &c.

SCENE I

In front of the great gate of the College. LYDIA's *house on
the left of the stage.*

CAIUS *and* BALBUS *in cap and gown.* HORACE *and* DECIUS
MUS *lounging in the back-ground.*

    Caius.—What time d'ye call it, Balbus? Why, good
      heaven,
I do declare it's only half-past seven !
And I was up last night till after two,
And lost—the Furies know how much—at loo.
As I was dreaming how you trumped my knave
The bell its matutinal warning gave :
Forth from his cosy bed the student shoots
Clad in a toga and a pair of boots,
Knocks down his soap-dish, blunders with his brushes,
And, half-undressed, to morning temple rushes.
    Balbus.—Caius, my worthy comrade—
    Cai.—   If you please
I very much prefer to be called Keys.
    Bal.—Well : who's that young Apulian? To my
      knowledge
I was on nodding terms with all the college.
    Cai.—That? Why, 'tis little Horace. Don't you
      know him ?
The same that got the Chancellor's Prize Poem ;
Who wears six rings, and curly as a maid is ;
Who's always humming songs about the ladies ;
Who never comes inside the gates till four ;
Who painted green the Senior Tutor's door.
I'll make you both acquainted. Here, my fuchsia,
This is the famous freshman from Venusia.
And this is Balbus, cleverest of dabs
At losing pewters and at catching crabs.

As to his antecedents, you must look
In the first page of Henry's Latin Book.
    Hor.—Can this be Balbus, household word to all,
Whose earliest exploit was to build a wall?
Who, with a frankness that I'm sure must charm ye,
Declared it was all over with the army.
Can this be he who feasted, as 'twas said,
The town at fifty sesterces a-head?
But, while the thankless mob his bounty quaffed,
Historians add—that there were some who laughed.
I should be deeply honoured if I might
Secure your presence at my rooms to-night.
A friend has sent me half-a-dozen brace
Of thrush and blackbird from a moor in Thrace.
These we will have for supper, with a dish
Of lobster-patties, and a cuttle-fish;
While those who have not dined in hall may rally O
Round that gigantic mess beginning galeo—
Lepado—temacho—and the Lord knows what.
You'll find it all in Liddell and in Scott.
    Bal.—A thousand thanks : the honour will be mine.
But our Dynamic lecture stands for nine.
Let's go to breakfast, Caius ; since I hate
To scald my mouth for fear of being late.
               [*Exeunt all but* HORACE *and* DECIUS MUS.
    Hor.—My Decius, since our earliest private school
You always were my fond and faithful fool.
I ate the blackberries : you scratched your legs.
I took the nests : you blew the addled eggs.
When we stole out at night to see the play
'Twas you, not I, who could not sit next day.
And now we live, a pair of trusty friends,
With common pleasures and with common ends.
To you, my Decius Mus, to you alone
I trust the secret that I burn to own.
Why is my colour gone, my visage lank?
Why did I steer our boat against the bank?

Why is my wine untasted in the glass ?
Why do I tremble when the proctors pass ?
By Proserpine below, by Jove above,
By mine own head I swear that I'm in love !

    Dec. M.—Don't swear so loud. I've not the slightest
        doubt of it.

I never knew the time when you were out of it.

    Hor.—'Tis true ! 'Tis true ! But this is not the same.
    So pure, so ardent, and so bright a flame !

Oh face ! oh form celestial !

    Dec. M.—   I knows her.

Quis multâ gracilis te, Pyrrha, in rosâ ?

    Hor.—Pyrrha, the faithless sorceress !

    Dec. M.—   Ah, I see !

Extremum Tanaim si biberes, Lyce.

Or her you told us of last night when beery,—

Die et argutæ properet Neæræ.

    Hor.—My sweetheart, Mus, outshines Neæra far

As D'Orsey's comet [1] beats the polar star.
Unkind as Lyce, and than Pyrrha giddier,
Whom can I mean but lovely lively Lydia ?

    Dec. M. [*aside*]—Perdition catch this fellow and his
        curls !

That such a doll as this should please the girls !
Lydia, my fondest hope, my only joy !
[*Aloud*] Horace, you're taken in this time, my boy !
Your darling Lydia is not all you think.
For a young lady she's a whale at drink :
And, though I don't believe the fact the least,
They say she went to the Olympian feast
In young Muræna's drag.

    Hor.   They lie—they lie !

They dared not breathe a word if I were by.

---

[1] In the year 1860 the Rev. Mr. D'Orsey obtained the Chancellor's medal for a poem on the Great Comet of 1858. This gentleman soon after became English lecturer at Corpus College, and commenced a course of instruction in clerical and public elocution : an undertaking in which the undergraduates of the day chose to discover something ludicrous.

I love her, though she's petulant and cruel,
As Radley boys adore the Reverend Sewell.
And now I've come to spend some anxious hours
Prostrate before her threshold, crowned with flowers.
Such was the custom, as good scholars know,
Of classic lovers long long time ago.
And if they doubt it, let them please to look
At my sixth line, ode twenty-fifth, first book ;
And as a penance let them learn by heart
The note by Anthon, and the verse by Smart.

Sings.

'Wake, O wake, my soul's enchantress !
Listen to your lover's pleadings.
Recognise in each effusion
Doctor Bentley's various readings.
Fair as golden Aphrodite ;
Piquante as Rebecca Sharpe ;
Worthy of the pen of Trollope ;
Theme for old Anacreon's harp ;
Colder than out-college breakfasts ; [1]
Harder than the Old Court stones ;
Beam upon me from the window ;
Have compassion on my groans.'
[HORACE *lies down on the threshold of* LYDIA's *house.*
LYDIA *opens the door, and stumbles over him.*

Lyd.—Plague take you, Horace ! See, you've torn my
gown.
Get up—and don't stay sprawling like the clown
Who lies with fiendish craft athwart the floor,
Then knocks at some unconscious tradesman's door.
Come, don't look like a fool, because you're not one.
But use your tongue :—at least if you have got one.

[1] The kitchen being within the Great Court, it is needless to describe the
condition in which stewed kidneys or curried fish arrive at lodgings distant
some half mile from the college gate.

N

Hor. [*Getting up*].—When like Diana's orb, serene and
     bright,
You rise resplendent on my aching sight,
My senses with a strange emotion swim,
And a cold shudder runs through every limb.
My eyes are dazzled, and my features glow,
As when a student in the Little-Go
Draws from his breast a surreptitious Paley,
Notes the contents, and floors the paper gaily ;
Then sees with horror in the gallery frowning
Some dread examiner from Cat's or Downing.

    Lyd.—What have you brought me, Horace ?   You shall
     rue
Unless it's something elegant and new.

    Hor.—Alas, my charmer, I have nought to bring.
I am too poor to buy a brooch or ring.

    Lyd.—Don't talk of brooches or of rings, you dove you,
'Tis for yourself, yourself alone, I love you.
Since I've been here I've had a hundred danglers,
Lords, fellow-commoners, and senior-wranglers,
Scholars, Smith's prizemen, deans, professors, dons,
Fellows of Trinity, and Queen's, and John's ;
But none like you, from all that brilliant throng,
I've loved so readily, or loved so long.
Your wit's so racy, and your words so glowing,
Your dress so spicy, and your wink so knowing ;
Your songs are better than ten thousand purses.
So run me off some amatory verses.
I'll be your critic :—and beware, I tell ye,
You'll find me worse than Hermann or Orelli.
But first we'll try one figure of the dance,
A thought pronounced, that Balbus learned in France,
(Confound my stupid head ! I mean in Gaul)
The year he brought me back my Cachmere shawl.
                        [*Dance. Exit* HORACE.

    Dec. M.—You faithless baggage, am I so much dirt,
That thus before my very nose you flirt ?

Have I not lain whole evenings at your door ?
My whole allowance spent, and hundreds more ?
Did I not bet my money on a screw
That I might lose four dozen gloves to you,
White kid and primrose, sixes and a quarter ?
Was it for this I jilted Gnatho's daughter ?
Was it for this I got on the committee,[1]
And sent you all my tickets ?   More's the pity !

   Lyd.—And if you did, though even that is false,
Did I not dance with you the fifteenth valse ?
And would have tried a galoppe with you gladly,
Except for very shame, you waltzed so badly.
You purchased me the gloves, (may harpies tear them !)
But what of that ?   I let you see me wear them.
Do what you will : your time and money waste :
But pray allow me to consult my taste.

   Dec. M.—For your sake, Lydia, while you still were mine,
They gated me for half the term at nine :
And for your sake uncounted sums I owe
To Gent and Matthew, Litchfield, Ingrey, Rowe.
And yet you still my hand and heart despise,
Won by the glances of a freshman's eyes.
You and your minion all your lives shall cuss
The day you played the fool with Decius Mus.

                                [*Exeunt.*

SCENE II

The Rooms of HORACE.

BALBUS, CAIUS, HORACE, *and others, at table.*

SONG

'Natis in usum lætitiæ.'—ODE XXVII. BOOK I.

To fight o'er cups for joy ordained
Suits well barbarian morals.
Let us our blushing Bacchus keep
From taint of bloody quarrels.

[1] The Committee of management of the Bachelors' Ball.

For Median daggers don't agree
With beer-cup rich and brown :
So rest your elbow on the couch,
And take your liquor down.

Come, drink about ! and, if you wish
That I should do the same,
I must request yon junior soph
To tell his sweetheart's name.

Bend close this way—Ah, wretched boy,
You're not her only suitor.
That lady has been long engaged
To our Assistant Tutor.

Dec. M.—Horace, your supper has been quite the thing.
You entertain as bravely as you sing.
I'm just three-quarters drunk, and tightly filled
With roast, and boiled, and stewed, and pulled, and grilled.
But there is one sad void within your doors,
One vacuum which nature most abhors.
For nought avails the spiced and bubbling bowl,
The pea in season, and the roe of sole,
Without fair woman, nature's proudest boast,
To pour the coffee and dispense the toast.
    Hor.—That shall be remedied, or Pluto's in it,
For I'm expecting Lydia every minute.
    Dec. M.—Things must be wonderfully changed of late
If she's allowed to pass the college gate.
I'll lay a mina on it.
    Hor.—   Done with you—
That she'll be here to-night.
    Dec. M.—   I'll make it two.

Sings—   *Enter* Lydia *disguised as a Bedmaker.*

    I make the butter fly, all in an hour :
        I put aside the preserves and cold meats,
    Telling my master his cream has turned sour,
        Hiding his pickles, purloining his sweets.

I never languish for husband or dower :
    I never sigh to see gyps at my feet :
I make the butter fly, all in an hour,
    Taking it home for my Saturday treat.

                            [Discovers herself.

Hor.   Well : Lydia dear, now you are here
        We'll have a game of loo, love ;
    Although I'm told the punch is cold
        With waiting long for you, love.
Lyd.   O, bother punch ! I've had my lunch,
        And afterwards some tea, love.
    A glass of sling is just the thing,
        And quite enough for me, love.

Enter SEMPRONIUS VIRIDIS, *a Freshman from Gallia
Cisalpina.*

Hor.—Behold the prototype of Verdant Green !
S.V.—Are these the chambers of the Junior Dean ?
Hor.—Sir, I'm the Junior Dean.
S.V.—   I wish to state
The reason of my coming rather late
To early lecture on last Friday week.
    Hor.—Young man, I bid you pause before you speak.
So grave a breach of college rules, by Castor.
Must come before no other than the Master.
In suppliant garb arrayed you'll duly call
Where stands his Lodge adjacent to the Hall.
There ask his pardon. If he chance to scold,
Back your entreaties with a piece of gold.

                    [SEMPRONIUS *begins to go.*

Stay for a moment ; let me ask your name.
    S.V.—Sempronius Viridis.
    Hor.—   The very same !

I knew your father.   Tell me, if you can,
Does he not look an oldish sort of man ?

S.V.—Yes, that he does.

Hor.—   I fancied I was right.
Hair grey, or now perhaps a little white ?
Sit down, and join our company, my boy,
Let's give an hour to chat and social joy.
The gravest of us now and then unbends,
And likes his glass of claret and his friends.

Caius.—But first, my dear Sempronius, pray let us
Inquire if you've ascended Mount Hymettus
To see the term divide—for, if I'm right,
That incident comes off this very night.

S.V.—Does it indeed !   I thank you from my heart.
If that's the case it's almost time to start.
I don't like walking late in cap and gown,
For fear of being beaten by the town.

> [CAIUS *removes his gown, and substitutes his own,*
> *which is old and ragged.   Dance expressive of re-*
> *monstrance on the part of* SEMPRONIUS, *and con-*
> *tempt on that of the others.   They hustle him out.*

Enter BRUTUS *and* CASSIUS *with Recruiting Ribbons.*

Hor.—Why here's two heroes coming to recruit us.
What is your business, pray ?

Bru.—   I'm Marcus Brutus :
And this is Caius Cassius, a name,
Thanks to Will Shakspere, not unknown to fame.
We found our country groaning, and to ease her
We sent to his account great Julius Cæsar.
But young Augustus with a hungry pack
Of veteran troops came yelping on my track ;
While Antony, more truculent by far,
Cries ' Havock ! ' and let slip the dogs of war.

There must be here some smart young fellows willing
To serve their country, and to take the shilling.
We stand the uniform.
 Hor.—   And what's the pay?
 Bru.—Your beer, and twenty sesterces a day.
Coffee you'll get, as green as any leaf,
Fat pork, hard biscuits, and nice fresh boiled beef.
The bounty will be paid as best it can,
For Brutus is an honourable man.
Then there's the glory, and the smiles of beauty,
And some one else to take your turn of duty.
Is there one true-born son of Rome who fears
To meet the shock of Cæsar's hireling spears,
With me to conquer, or with me to die?
If any, speak! I pause for a reply.
 All.—None, Brutus, none.
 Bru.—   Then none have I offended.
But now we'll go! 'Tis time this scene were ended.
We start to-morrow, by Apollo's grace,
On the main route for Macedon and Thrace.
So get your kits packed up, and don't be late.
The convoy's due at seven fifty-eight.

          [*Exeunt omnes.*

SCENE III

The Senate-House. Augustus, Mæcenas, *the* Vice-Chancellor, *the* Public Orator, Decius Mus, Lydia,
Students *in the Gallery, etc.*

 V. C.—Your Royal Highness, wearied with the jars
Of civil discord and intestine wars,
Has for a while withdrawn you from the strife
To taste the sweets of Academic life:
And we have done our utmost to prepare
A varied and enticing bill of fare.

First, with absorbing interest you'll see
Mæcenas take an honorary degree.
Next, Decius Mus—of whom we're justly proud,
A youth with parts and modesty endowed,
On whom our fondest expectations hang—
Will speak a complimentary harangue :
Which will be followed by a feast in hall,
Succeeded by a supper and a ball.

   Aug.—Think you that to a fool I've such affinity
As to consent to dine in hall in Trinity ?
I thank you for the kindness that you show ;
And in return this favour I bestow.
In honour of my uncle I will found
A Julian scholarship worth sixty pound.
Examiners,—the lecturer on Greek,
The preacher at St. Mary's for the week,
The last Seatonian prizeman, and the Deans
Of Pembroke, Corpus, Sidney, Christ's, and Queen's.
They will examine, such are my intentions,
In plane astrology of three dimensions.   [*Applause.*
And in return, for purposes of state,
I shall make bold to take the college plate,
And lay a tax of ninety-nine per cent.
On all the fellows' stipends and the rent.

                              [*Great sensation.*
And now we will proceed, if so you please,
At once to the conferring of degrees.

PUBLIC ORATOR *leads up* MÆCENAS.

   Pub. Or.—Præsento tibi hunc baccalaureum, cui re-
servatur sua senioritas.   [*Cheering.*

   V. C.—Mæcenas, vir amplissime, edite atavis regi-
bus, O et præsidium et dulce decus nostrum, confirmo
tibi tuam senioritatem. Neque dubitari potest, vir
reverende atque doctissime, quin si natum haberem tuo

ingenio præditum, omnes omnia bona dicerent, et
laudarent fortunas meas—

STUDENTS *in the Gallery.*

Three cheers for Caius Cæsar !
Three groans for Mr. Bright !
And now, in hopes to please her,
Three cheers for the lady in white !
Hurrah for the 'Varsity boat !
Hurrah for Robinson's vote !

V. C.—Since classic phrases pall on minds so weak,
'Tis time for Decius Mus to rise and speak !
Dec. M.—Let me unfold before your royal ear
The doings of the Academic year.
Religious education and sound knowledge
Have flourished generally throughout the college :
Although the chapel-clerks, astounding fact,
For every surplice seven-and-six exact.
The porters too, who really should know better,
Charge us a halfpenny for every letter.[1]
The fellowships have gone, save one in three,
In inverse ratio to the degree :
And we expect next year a junior op
Will, by the aid of bookwork, come out top.[2]
We've a hall steward, who becomes the place,
And draws his salary with wondrous grace :
But no one can perceive, as I'm a sinner,
A very marked improvement in the dinner.

[1] This impost dated from the time when the postage of letters was heavy,
and demanded a plentiful store of cash and careful accounts on the part of
the officer whose business it was to take in the correspondence of a numerous
body of people, most of whom could read and write with ease.   Those who
have the principal interest in the question—the porters themselves—credit
the couplet with the abolition of the tax.

[2] In the first edition the above four lines, the dearest the writer ever
penned, were suppressed at the last moment, and fresh matter substituted.
But a thrifty bookbinder used the rejected pages to strengthen the covers of
a certain number of copies : so that the reader could gratify his curiosity
by the simple process of holding up the binding to the light.   Few could be
induced to believe that the author was not a party to this suicidal policy.

We still consume, with mingled shame and grief,
Veal that is tottering on the verge of beef;
Veal void of stuffing, widowed of its ham,
Or the roast shoulder of an ancient ram.
Illustrious founder of a mighty line,
Go forth, and seize the sceptre that is thine !
Thou who hast studied in thine uncle's school :
For he did rear a race he might not rule,
(Although he paid for it uncommon dear) :
So thou shalt rule a race thou didst not rear.[1] [*Applause.*

   Aug.—Upon my word, young man, you make me
      proud,
Although you need not bellow quite so loud.
So well you've learnt your speech, so nicely said it,
It does yourself and your instructors credit.
And therefore, in return, I'll not refuse
Whatever boon you ask. Look sharp and choose.
   Dec. M.—Then will your highness get me back, I
      pray,
A female slave of mine who's run away ?
There stands the wench, blue-girdled round the waist.
   Aug.—By Hercules, this Decius Mus has taste.
Well, since you say she's yours in justice, take her ;
And if she won't go with you—why, I'll make her.
   Lyd.—Sir, I entreat you by her name that bore you,
By that dear maid whose beaming eyes adore you,
Save me, O save me, from that bitter fate,
To be betrayed to one I scorn and hate.
I hate him, for he's rude, untidy, black,
In debt to Parfitt, Warwicker, and Flack.

---

  [1] These lines were a parody on a passage well known at the time, occurring in the prize poem on the subject of ' The Prince of Wales at the tomb of Washington ' :

      ' For he did rear a race he might not rule.
      So thou shalt rule a race thou didst not rear.'

The university lyre, which for long past had given forth very feeble strains, was just then falling into the hands of a Cheltenham freshman, Mr. Frederick Myers, who in this performance gave promise that has been worthily fulfilled in the all too little which he has hitherto given to the world.

To sum up all, deny it if he can,
A jealous, hideous, odious ten-year man.

Aug.—Take off the girl !
Lyd.— Oh, Sire !
Aug.— Have done, I say !
I can't be waiting here the livelong day.

[LYDIA *is dragged off. Scene changes.*

SCENE IV

In front of BRUTUS'S *Tent.*

HORACE *on guard. Enter* CAIUS.

Cai.—Horace, my boy, I thought I heard you singing,
And so I've come, these slight refreshments bringing.
We'll drain a bumper to your absent Lydia,
The sweetest girl from Britain to Pisidia.
And that reminds me. Some one in the band
Has brought a letter, in a female hand,
Addressed to you : an obol to be paid.

[CAIUS *delivers the letter.*

Hor.—There's something wrong with Lydia, I'm afraid.
What's this ? [*Reads.*] ' My Horace, 'tis not yet too late
To save your darling from a dreadful fate.
The fatal time draws nigh. Haste, haste, and save ! '

[*Dashes down the letter.*

Shall Lydia be my faithless rival's slave ?
Caius, 'tis now the time to come down handsome :
You shall provide the money for her ransom.

Cai.—But all my ready cash has gone in liquor
For your consumption. *Hor.*— Well then, pawn your ticker.

Cai.—But why not pawn your own ?

Hor.— Oh, heartless friend,
Your selfish words my tender bosom rend.

Was it for this I loved you as myself?
Was it for this I freely shared your pelf?
Was it for this your board I nightly graced,
And criticized your wines with faultless taste?

Sings.

We were fresh together.
    I never can forget
How in October weather
    On Parker's Piece we met ;
Nor how in hall we paid so dear
    For shapeless lumps of flesh,
And sized for cheese and college beer,
    When you and I were fresh.

We were Junior Sophs together,
    And used one Paley card.[1]
They plucked my every feather,
    A usual fate, but hard.
You got the Craven and the Bell,
    While I in folly's mesh
Without a single struggle fell,
    When you and I were fresh.

We're Questionists together ;
    We both have reached the verge
And limit of our tether,
    The hood of fur and serge,

[1] The card alluded to was an epitome of *The Evidences of Christianity*, which work formed one among the subjects of the Little-go examination. In this synopsis doctrinal arguments were summed up in rude Hexameters and Pentameters for the assistance of treacherous memories. The eleven proofs of the authenticity of the Historical Scriptures were contained in the lines :

    Quoted, sui generis, vols, titles, publicly, comment,
    Both sides, without doubt, attacked, catalogue, apocryphal.

The learning by heart of this barbarous jargon was an important element in that religious training, on the pretext of preserving which inviolate the yearly bills for admitting nonconformists to the privileges and emoluments of our universities have been talked out of the Commons or kicked out of the Lords.

Though this should be a Federal firm,
 And that a hot Secesh,
We'd fondly still recall the term
 When you and I were fresh.

Enter BRUTUS, *at the head of his army.*

Bru.—Halt ! Right face ! 'tention ! Don't be crowd-
 ing there !
You seem to think we're forming hollow square.
Now, since this neighbourhood is somewhat damp,
To-morrow morning we shall strike our camp,
And, having marched some twenty miles with unction,
Take up our ground beyond Philippi junction.
When the first beams of Sol the meadows kiss,
Be all of you prepared to start. Dis-miss !
      [*Exeunt all but* BRUTUS.

The Stage grows dark.

There's nothing stirring all along the line.
Boy, place a chair, and bring a flask of wine.
I'll sit awhile alone, and drown my sorrow,
And think about my tactics for to-morrow.
   [*Sits and sips. Ghost of* CÆSAR *rises, to music.*
Unless I'm wrong, this Massic's rather fruity.
I'll have another bottle.
 Ghost.—   Et tu, Brute !

SONG AND DANCE.

 I shrink from the light,
 But at dead of night
In a ghastly polka skip I :
 And all this way
 I've come to say
That I'll meet you again at Philippi.

Bru.　　　　　I very much rue
　　　　　That I ran you through,
　　　I've been a terrible rip, I :
　　　　　But please, Sir, don't,
　　　　　I hope you won't
　　　Ever meet me again at Philippi.

Ghost.　　　　By the light of the moon
　　　　　I have come full soon
　　　All armed with Tisiphone's whip, I :
　　　　　Your sins shall be lashed,
　　　　　And your hopes all dashed,
　　　When I meet you again at Philippi.
　　　　　　　　　　　　[*Exeunt dancing.*

SCENE V

The Plains of Philippi. BRUTUS *and* CASSIUS, *at the head
of their army.*

Bru.—Cassius, the fatal hour is drawing nigh.
The time has come to conquer or to die.
That veteran force at which you daily scoff
Is marching to the fight some furlongs off :
While all our three-months' volunteers go home,
And meet a cordial welcome back to Rome.
'Tis time to form my soldiers for the fight.
Fall in !　Attention !　Number from the right !
　　　[*That manœuvre takes place with the usual success.
　　　The Army marches out. Alarms. Excursions.
　　　The Army rushes in again in confusion.*

Enter QUINTUS RUSSELLUS MAXIMUS.

Rus.—What means this most discreditable bustle ?
I am the correspondent, Quintus Russell.
Describe the enemy, that I may draw him.
Sol.—We can't describe him, for we never saw him.

Rus.—You never saw the foe ! This is indeed
A most confused, unsoldierlike stampede.
I never met with such a shameful scene,
As daily correspondent though I've been
(At least I doubt if you will find a dailyer)
In every fight from Munda to Pharsalia.
My military knowledge is not small.
I witnessed Cæsar's first campaign in Gaul,
And found myself in an unpleasant mess
For making known his tactics through the press.
The late reforms, as e'en the Horse-guards own,
Are due to me, and due to me alone.
Give me the standard ! On to martial deeds !
None dare turn craven when their critic leads !
This foul dishonour from your annals wipe !
Whoever runs shall read his name in type.

Sol.—Now by our free and most enlightened nation
We'll teach this Britisher to know his station.
We are afraid of being killed, 'tis true :
But strike me blind if we're afraid of you !
We'll tar and feather you from head to tail,
And ride you round the country on a rail.
Scene-painter, lend us all your brushes, pray.
We'll take our chance of what the ' Times ' may say.

[*They seize* QUINTUS RUSSELLUS MAXIMUS.

Enter CASSIUS *and* BRUTUS.

Rus.—Release me, Brutus ! In the English press
I'll say you gained a glorious success.
I will indeed ! Or, if it suit you better,
You shall yourself compose to-morrow's letter.
Stain not your spotless name with useless crimes !
O save the correspondent of the ' Times ' !

Bru.—Forbear, my soldiers ! For 'tis most absurd
To make a correspondent like a bird.

Protect the baggage, lest their stragglers loot us.

[*Exeunt* SOLDIERS.

Fly, stranger, fly, and bless the name of Brutus !

[*Exit* QUINTUS RUSSELLUS MAXIMUS.

All hope is faded.   Cassius, be not weak.
Fate closes in.   Together must we seek
That undiscovered country from whose bourn
No uncommercial travellers return.
Present thy sword, and when I give the sign
Fall on my point, and I will fall on thine.

Cas.—Ah, Brutus, this fond faithful heart will burst.
I love you far too well to die the first :
But when I've mourned thy death with many a groan
I'll bid thy life-blood mingle with mine own.

Bru.—Well, be it so.   Hold out the fatal blade.
One ! two ! three ! Off ! Confound it, who's afraid ?

[*Rushes on the sword, and falls.*

This was the way I died, but they relate, O,
That I was murdered by my freedman Strato.

[*Dies.   Cassius takes his purse, and runs off with an air of relief.*

Enter HORACE *humming.*

Hor.—The minstrel-boy from the wars is gone,
          And out of breath you'll find him ;
He has run some five miles off and on,
          And his shield has flung behind him.
I hope this spot is out of range of fire.
Why ! here's the general prostrate in the mire,
Dead as a stoker on the Brighton line !
Speak, my lord Brutus ! Speak ! He gives no sign.
Woe worth the day ! Woe worth this fatal field !
I've lost my leader, thrown away my shield.
My mother charged me, as she tied her bonnet,
To come back either with it or upon it.

My honour could endure no worse disaster
Unless I voted for myself as Master.
I'm sure I heartily repent, by Juno.
Quo mihi pareret legio Romana tribuno.   [*Exit.*

SCENE VI

The head-quarters of AUGUSTUS, *near Philippi.*

AUGUSTUS, MÆCENAS, DECIUS MUS, LYDIA, HORACE *in custody*, SOLDIERS, GUARDS, ETC.

Soldier.—My Lord, while foraging the country round,
Our skirmishers this prisoner have found ;
Who, by his gallant mien and splendid coat,
We guess will prove an officer of note.
He ran so quickly from the scene of strife
That his must be a valuable life.
   Aug.—So young, and yet a rebel !   Oh, for shame !
Are any here acquainted with his name ?
   Dec. M.—This wretched youth, a nursling of sedition,
At Athens College holds an exhibition,
Which would have gone to me, without a doubt,
Had but the founder's will been carried out.
When Rome your highness for her consul chose
He ventured at the Union to propose
' That this assembly views with reprobation
' A measure fraught with danger to the nation.'
A motion which, although opposed by me,
Was passed by eighty votes to twenty-three.
And in his ode, conceive it if you can, Sir,
He dared insert a most Horatian stanza
Which speaks of Tully as our forum's pride,
A man he knows your highness can't abide.
   Aug.—Enough, his guilt is proved, at least to me.
Rig up a gallows on the nearest tree !

o

What, in reply to all we just have heard,
Can you allege that sentence be deferred?
   Hor.—My loved protector, patron kind and true
Of hapless genius, I appeal to you,
To you, Mæcenas, sprung from royal stock,
My sweetest glory, and my guardian rock.
There are whom it delights with wondrous gust
To have collected the Olympic dust—
   Mæc.—Perhaps so, but I can't discover quite
How that will help you in your present plight.
Unless your circumstances greatly alter
You're much more likely to collect a halter.
Augustus, spare this most unlucky lad
Who's far too idle to be very bad.
He sings a sparkling song, can write a bit,
And boasts some talent, impudence, and wit.
He's asked to every supper in the town ;
He got a Camden, and he halved a Browne ; [1]
And, as a coping-stone to all his praise,
He took a seventh class in both his Mays.
   Aug.—Well, if this budding hero is a poet,
We soon will find some means to make him show it.
To 'scape the consequences of your frolic.
Be pleased to parody the tenth Bucolic.

   Hor.—What haunts detain you on this ill-starred day,
      Castalian Muses, say ? [2]
What seat of classic lore, what hallowed stream ?
      Strayed you by sedgy Cam,
      While from the Barnwell dam
You watch the gambols of the silver bream ?

---

[1] Of late years the Browne medal for Latin and Greek epigrams had been divided between the successful competitors in the respective languages : to the annual disgust of both the half-medallists ; each of whom, with the partiality of an author, regarded himself as having lost by the change of system.

[2]   ' Quæ nemora aut qui vos saltus habuere, puellæ Naiades,' &c.

Or by the willows weeping
O'er Cherwell slowly creeping
Swoll'n with the suds of many an ancient hall
Past Jowett's cloistered cell and Stanley's stall?
Or have ye flown, invoked in boyish song,
    To Harrow's far-seen hill?
    Or hard by Avon's rill
Beloved of Hughes the earnest and the strong,
And along Barby-road, and round the Island Goal,
And Caldecott's famed spinney do ye stroll
    On this unhappy morn
When fair Venusia's tuneful swain
Trembling all in captive chain
With drooping eyes endures the victor's scorn?—

Aug.—Well done! You really have a turn for
    rhyme.
I think we'll hear the rest another time.
Mæcenas, you'll impress on him, I hope,
How very narrowly he missed the rope.
I'll give your protegé, still more to pleasure ye,
A nomination in the public Treasury.
So be prepared to pass, on this day week,
In hydrostatics, German, French, and Greek,
One eastern language, botany, precis,
(I don't exactly know what that may be,
Nor do I long to probe the fearful mystery,)
Pure mathematics, law, and modern history.
And as for Decius Mus,—well, stop a bit,
I think I know a post for which he's fit,
(Unless indeed our partial feelings warp us ;)—
I'll make him English lecturer at Corpus,
There let him work a total revolution
In Clerical and Public Elocution.
    Hor.—My lord Augustus, by the Gods above,
    This one prayer grant me! Give me back my
      love.

Without my Lydia life itself is loss,
And Treasury clerkships seem but so much dross.
Restore my darling ! Well your poet knows
To pay what debt of gratitude he owes.
    Aug.—Let mistress Lydia pick, and pray make haste,
Whiche'er of these two fellows suits her taste.
Our judgment shall be guided by her voice ;
I cannot say I envy her the choice.

' Donec gratus eram tibi.'—ODE IX. BOOK III.

Hor. While still you loved your Horace best
      Of all my peers who round you pressed,
      (Though not in expurgated versions)
      More proud I lived than King of Persians.

Lyd. And while as yet no other dame
      Had kindled in your breast a flame,
      (Though Niebuhr her existence doubt)
      I cut historic Ilia out.

Hor. Dark Chlöe now my homage owns,
      With studied airs, and dulcet tones ;
      For whom I should not fear to die,
      If death would pass my charmer by.

Lyd. I now am lodging at the rus-
      In-urbe of young Decius Mus.
      Twice over would I gladly die
      To see him hit in either eye.

Hor. But should the old love come again,
      And Lydia her sway retain ?
      If to my heart once more I take her,
      And bid dark Chlöe wed the baker ?

Lyd.   Though you be treacherous as audit [1]
        When at the fire you've lately thawed it,
        For Decius Mus no more I'd care
        Than for their plate the Dons of Clare.[2]

Aug.—In that case, whether you prefer or not,
I must insist you take her on the spot.
I'll give you, won by her transcendent charms,
The choicest of your patron's Sabine farms.
There shall you live 'midst garlands, wine, and rhymes,
The darling of your own and future times ;
And be translated, as a poet should,
In prose by Watson and in verse by Good.

Hor.   O the heavenly bliss
                Of that first long kiss,
            As in my arms I locked her ;
                When none need shout,
                ' You fool look out,
            ' Here comes the Senior Proctor ! '

Aug.   Light Hymen's torch,
                And deck the porch !
            May smiling Venus bless you !
                May Chian flow,
                And roses blow,
            And critics ne'er distress you !

---

[1] Connoisseurs treat audit ale like claret, and place it for a while in front of the fire : but the effect is seldom ascertained ; for the corks (such corks, at any rate, as fall to the portion of gentlemen in statu pupillari) almost invariably leap from the bottles, and are followed by the best part of the ale.

[2] About this period the authorities of Clare College took it into their heads to sell at the price of old silver some fine plate, said to have been presented to their predecessors immediately after the Restoration in order to replace that which had been sacrificed in darker times to the royal cause. The proceeding excited in virtuoso circles a good deal of contemptuous astonishment.

Hor.
       But now 'tis late,
       The college gate
Has long been shut, I'm certain.
       So thus, kind friends,
       Our story ends,
And we must drop the curtain.

THE CAMBRIDGE DIONYSIA :

A Classic Dream

[In the year 1858 there appeared at Cambridge the *Lion*, a magazine very creditably conducted, written chiefly or entirely by undergraduates. It displayed Transcendental tendencies, which, combined with the belief that some of the contributors knew a good deal of German and the certainty that others knew very little Latin, excited the bitter wrath of those young men who aspired to classical honours, and among them of the author, who parodied the first number in a performance entitled the *Bear*. A second number of the obnoxious publication soon followed, and produced the ' Cambridge Dionysia,' which was written in a frenzy of boyish indignation. The *Lion* survived this renewed assault, and got eventually into a third number :—which for a University periodical may be considered an instance of longevity.

The prose portion of the ' Dionysia ' was written for a circle of readers who were obliged from the necessities of their position annually to make themselves masters of the smallest details in the celebration of the Bacchic festivals ; and may still amuse such of them as retain their hold on the main outlines of that somewhat unprofitable field of knowledge. The verse is in imitation of an Athenian Comedy. Whether it be that the author's mind was at the time more Greek than English :—or that Cambridge society was so limited as to admit of the personal allusions being generally intelligible, and, if truth be told, rather scurrilous :—or that the style and tone of a writer are most readily assimilated by those at his own period of life ; (and, according to the received chronology, the great poet produced the Knights and the Acharnians while emerging from his teens) :—from some or all of these causes it happens that this trifle, while most inadequately representing the humour, the vigour, the fertility, the exquisite fancy of the comedian, faithfully enough reproduces his mannerism. Among the more superficial Aristophanic qualities which the ' Dionysia ' reflects may be included a wilful ignorance of the subjects satirised. The author was at least as hopelessly unacquainted with the notions of Emerson as Aristophanes was with the tenets of Socrates : whose teaching he supposed to consist in natural history, for which the philosopher had a strong distaste, and in forensic rhetoric, for which he entertained an intense and immortal aversion.

The plot, and much of the text, are in pretty close paraphrase of the ' Wasps ' :—a drama widely known in the modern and rather awkward dress of Racine's ' Plaideurs.' By a fortunate chance the names of the two principal characters in the original play required nothing but the insertion of a single letter to adapt them for Cambridge use : and Philoleon answers to the Athenian dotard who is placed under tutelage by his own son, with feelings embittered by the reflection that he is ' an only father.' Happy time, when an undergraduate in his last year of residence seemed an impersonation of old age !]

TRINITY COLLEGE, *November*, 1858.

ON the first Audit-day of this year Shillibere, with whom I was engaged upon the Wasps of Aristophanes,

told me that as it was the πιθοιγία[1] he would excuse
my reading with him, but bade me get up the subject
of the Dionysiac festivals against our next meeting. I
took a longer walk than was my wont, and by hall-time
was quite ready to appreciate the fact of its being a
Feast. After dinner Barlow, the Bachelor Scholar,
came to my rooms, and we sat late, drinking sherry,
and discussing the merits of the ale at the different
colleges. When he had gone I took down the Wasps,
but somehow or other I could not make much of them.
So I drew my easy-chair to the fire, filled my pipe, and
opened Smith's Antiquities on the article ' Dionysia.'
But the Greek words bothered me, and I was too lazy
to rise for a Lexicon. So I fell a thinking on Athens,
and what glorious fun the festival must have been. I
can recollect nothing more till I found myself in the
midst of a strange dream. And yet, marvellous as it
was, nothing seemed to surprise me ; but I took it
for granted that everything was perfectly natural and
consistent. And the dream was as follows :

I was still sitting in my rooms with my books before
me : but it was broad daylight, and a lovely morning,
such as sometimes breaks upon us, even at Cambridge,
in the beginning of November. The courts were very
quiet, but I heard a constant shouting in the distance,
as if there was some tumult in the streets. Suddenly
the door flung open, and Barlow appeared. He looked
flushed and excited ; on his head was a garland of ivy-
leaves, and he swung in his hand a pewter. ' Shut up
your books,' he cried : ' no reading on the πιθοιγία.
If you do another equation I'll inform against you for

---

[1] The classic mind of the great coach might well find an analogy between
the day in the rubric of old Athens which derived its name from the opening
of the casks to taste the wine of the preceding year, and the day in the
calendar of modern Trinity when by solemn custom the fresh brew of
college ale flows in mediæval abundance. [In fact Shilleto used πιθοιγία
for the Trinity Audit Feast in his letter to my father printed p. 42 above,—
a letter subsequent to the appearance of this passage in the Cambridge
Dionysia.]

impiety. The God, the jolly God, hates Colenso worse than he hated Pentheus. I've come to fetch you to the theatre, whether you will or no. There is a new comedy to be represented, and all the University will be there. By Hercules, I hope they'll hit the authorities hard. When the performance is over we sup with Rumbold of Caius, culinary Caius, the head-quarters of good living. I am king of the feast, and not a soul shall get off under three bottles. We have stolen the chaplets from the Botanical Gardens; Ingrey sends the dessert, and Stratton has promised to bring two flute-players from Barn——.' Here I started up, crying, 'Barlow, lead on! I'm your man.' And we danced out of the New Court gate, and up the lane into Trinity-street. And there was a sight that made my heart leap.

The whole road was crowded with men, all in the wildest state of joy and liquor. Every one acknowledged the presence of the God, to whom liberty and license are dear. Laughing, singing, cheering, jesting, they were pouring in an unbroken stream towards Magdalene-bridge. Gyps mingled with the throng, enjoying perfect freedom and equality on this day of the year. Ever and anon some fresh band of revellers issued from the colleges and lodging-houses on the way, and swelled the main flood. Here came a mob of Queens' men, sweeping the street, and roaring at the pitch of their voices, 'For he's a jolly good fellow:' referring probably to the late senior wrangler. There, from the great gate of Harry the Eighth, streamed forth the whole club of Third Trinity. In front, arm-in-arm, strode the victorious four; while elevated on the shoulders of the crew of the second boat sat the secretary, his temples crowned with roses, riding a huge barrel, and bearing in his hand a silver bowl foaming with cider-cup. As we passed All Saints'-passage, from the direction of the Hoop Inn there moved a goodly company, twenty-five or thirty in number, and my companion whispered to me that this was the Historical Society,[1] and bawled out to them to ask whether Elizabeth was justified in putting Mary to death. And just inside the gateway of St. John's College there was a group of young men who successively tried to dance on an inflated pigskin. And he who danced best received a draught of their ale. And presently there came by a drunken Trinity sizar, who, after a successful trial, took the flagon, but when he had tasted, he cursed, and spit, and swore no Trinity shoe-black would condescend to drink it. Upon which a stout Johnian kicked his shins, and, as it was evident that trouble would ensue, and that we as men of the same College would be implicated in it, we hurried away, not wishing to desecrate the festival of the God by evil feelings. And on Magdalene-bridge was seated a knot of idle fellows who chaffed all the passers-by. And among others they told a solitary individual in a Downing-gown that he was so few that his College did not think it worth its while to brew for him, but had sent out for a gallon of swipes from the Eagle for his special consumption. So at last we arrived at the gate of the theatre, and after paying threepence each, which had been furnished us from the University Chest, we went in and sat down.

One side of the Castle-hill had been hollowed out into a spacious theatre. Tier above tier the long benches rose to the summit of the slope. In the front seats were the Vice-chancellor, and the heads of colleges, and doctors of divinity, and professors, and noblemen, and all who could claim founders' kin. And the rest of the space was filled to overflowing with undergraduates and bachelors. But all females were excluded from the

[1] The Historical Society took its rise at a time when the debates at the Union had given such an impulse to oratory that men were found who thought once a week not often enough for discussing to what extent Hampden was legally authorised in resisting the imposition of ship-money, and whether Addison or the Duke of Marlborough most deserved the admiration of posterity.

spectacle. And the throng was very clamorous, and many were provided with oranges, and nuts, and even stones, wherewith to pelt the unpopular actors. And in the orchestra was an altar, at which Shillibere stood, crowned with ivy, and robed in a long white robe. And from time to time he poured copious libations of ale upon the ground.[1]

All this I saw, and much more. And next me sat a staid bachelor, who seemed as if he had taken no part in the jollity of the morning. So we fell into conversation, and he told me how the theatre had been built under the inspection of Dr. Donaldson, from a comparison of plans furnished by freshmen in the Trinity College examinations. And he said that the festival of this year was jovial beyond any that had preceded it ; for that the public mind had just recovered from the painful excitement caused by the mutilation of the statues on the roof of Trinity library : which act men had suspected to be part of a plot for overturning the constitution of the University, and delivering us over to the Commissioners. And that report said there would be two Choruses in this play. And that fourteen First Trinity jerseys had been ordered from Searle's, and one of great size for the Coryphæus. And he would have said more, but a tipsy Pembroke man bade him hold his tongue, or he would bring against him an action of sacrilege at the next private business meeting in the Union, for disturbing the worship of the God. So we looked, and the curtain had already been drawn down. And the scene disclosed was in the Old Court of Trinity, letter Z ; and two gyps were asleep outside the door ; and the clock struck six, and first one started up, and then the other.

Gyp A.—I dreamed we both were waiting in the Hall Serving refreshments at the Bachelors' Ball.

[1] See p. 42 above, Shilleto's letter and note.

There, gayest trifler in the throng of dancers,
Was Clayton [1] cutting figures in the Lancers.

Gyp B.—Well dreamt ! But I have dreams as fine as
you.
Here's one as marvellous, and just as true.
Methought I heard our Rhadamanthine Mayor
Deal justice from the magisterial chair.
A Corpus sizar had been well-nigh slain
By fifteen blackguards in St. Botolph's Lane.
The Mayor approved his fellow-townsmen's pluck,
And fined the plaintiff two-pound-ten for luck.
As pensively he rubbed his broken head,
' Confound old Currier Balls ! ' the gownsman said.[2]

Gyp A.—Come now, I'll chat a little with the
audience.
Our master here, who keeps in the top-story,
Honest Philoleon, for his first three years
Led a most quiet and gentlemanly life.
He was not gated more than twice a term ;
He read three hours a-day, rode every week ;
Last year pulled seven in our second boat.
In all things moderation was his motto.
But now he's gone stark mad ; and you must guess
What sort his madness is.[3]   [*To the spectators.*

Gyp B.—That Queens' man there
Says that he's bent on being senior wrangler.[4]

[1] This gentleman preached an annual sermon against the Bachelors' Ball :
a festival about which reading men talked a great deal, but at which they
would as soon have thought of appearing as Mr. Clayton himself.

[2] In this autumn frequent collisions occurred between the boating-men
of the University and the police. The most obnoxious member of the force
was a certain 20 C, or 20 K, who is more than once alluded to in the course
of this Drama. Mr. Balls, the Mayor for the time being, had pretty
constantly to sit in judgment on cases of assault and battery.

[3]   ἐπεὶ τοπάζετε.
'Αμυνίας μὲν ὁ Προνάπου φησ' οὑτοσὶ
εἶναι φιλόκυβον αὐτόν· κ. τ. λ.—*Wasps*, line 73.

[4] Queens' college carried off the blue riband in the years 1857 and 1858,
in the person of champions who, according to the gossip of the senate-house,
were by some years senior to their competitors.

Gyp A.—No, no ; he won't be old enough these ten
years.

Gyp B.—And that black-whiskered noisy party yonder,
Sitting amongst a group of Harrow freshmen,[1]
Guesses he aims at office in the Union.

Gyp A.—What, to be called united and compact,
And to be chaffed in the suggestion book ?
Not quite so low as that.   Come, try again.
D'ye give it up ?   Well, listen, and I'll tell you.
One Sunday evening last May term at tea
He met by chance a troop of roaring Lions,
And came back swearing he must join their number,
Or give up hopes of immortality.
From that day forth he ran about the college,
Talking of ' Truth,' and ' Realised Ideals ' ;
And asking men to give him a $\pi o\hat{v} \sigma\tau\hat{\omega}$; [2]
And telling them he saw within their eyes
Symptoms which marked affinity of souls.
So, in this state of things, his younger brother
Bdelyleon came up this term to College,
A sensible sharp-tempered Eton freshman ;
Who, when he saw his brother's strange distemper,
Blushed for himself and for the family.
And first he tried by pleasing the old fellow
To wean him from his hobby ;   taught him songs,
And took him out to supper :   but whenever
His health was drunk, and he was asked to sing,

---

[1] During the spring of 1858 a ministerial crisis occurred in the Union
Society.   The official element had become unpopular among the mass of
the boating-men : whom in their turn the bureaucracy stigmatised by the
epithet of ' the bargees.'   The most noisy orator of the opposition was a
Harrow freshman : who, upon one occasion, began a withering peroration
with the words ' there they sit, compact, united ' : indicating at the same
time the Government bench by a sweep of the arm :   an amount of gesticula-
tion so unprecedented within those walls as to convulse the audience with
emotion.   Party spirit at length ran so high, and the attendance was consequently so large, that a stand-and-fall division was taken in the neighbouring auction rooms ; the Union itself having become nearly as uncomfortable
as the House of Commons on an ordinary business night.

[2] ' Give us a $\pi o\hat{v} \sigma\tau\hat{\omega}$, and we will move the world.'—Extract from the
Preface to the *Lion*.

He spoke straight off a canto from ' St. Clair.' [1]
And then he dressed him in his best, and washed
    him,
And got him made a member of the Musical :
But, at the first rehearsal, off he ran,
His fiddle on his back, and never stopped
Till he was inside Palmer's Printing-office.
So, vexed and wearied at his constant folly,
The young one locked him up within his rooms,
And placed us here on sentry, day and night.
But the old chap is sly, and full of tricks,
And loves his liberty.

                [PHILOLEON *appears at the window.*

  Phil.—Hallo, you scoundrel !
Just let me out : 'tis time to go to lecture.

  Gyp A.—Why you're a questionist : you have no
    lectures.

                [*Enter* BDELYLEON.

  Bdel.—Was ever freshman plagued with such a
    brother ?
What have I done that I deserve this evil ?
I never was undutiful ; I never
Have read a line of Alexander Smith ;
Nor picked a pocket ; nor worn peg-top trousers ;
Nor taken notes at any college lecture.
Who calls dame Fortune blind does not bely her.

  Phil.—I want a supper order from my tutor.

  Bdel.—No, no, old boy, I took good care of that :
I got you an ægrotat. Sold again !
Where are you now ? Good heavens !

        [PHILOLEON *puts his head out of the chimney.*

  Phil.   I'm the smoke.[2]

---

[1] A poem in Octosyllabics, entitled ' St. Clair,' was among the contributions to the *Lion*, which was published by Mr. Palmer.

[2]   οὗτος, τίς εἶ σύ ;
      καπνὸς ἔγωγ' ἐξέρχομαι.—*Wasps*, line 144.

Bdel.—Confound the man who altered all our chimneys !

Jackson, run up, and beat him with the pewter
Till he backs water ; then clap on a sack.

[PHILOLEON *reappears at the window.*

Phil.—O Lord St. Clair, on bended knee
I charge you set the maiden free !
Bdel.—In mercy stop that nonsense quick.
Your Lion always makes me sick.
I feel as ill as when I tried
My first and only Smoker's Pride.

Phil.—O may the curses of the Gods light on you !
And may you wallow in the lowest Hades,
Along with all the men who've struck their Tutor,
Or laid against the boat-club of their College,
Or caught a crab just opposite the Plough :
In that sad place of punishment and woe
Where lectures last from early dawn till noon,
And where the gate-fines rival those at Christ's,
And there's a change of Proctors every week ! [1]
Then you'll repent of having used me thus.

Bdel.—You blasphemous old villain ! Come, you fellows,
We all must need some coffee this cold morning.

[*Enter Chorus of writers of the ' Lion,' preceded by a chorister bearing a lantern.*

Chorus A.—Rosy-fingered dawn is breaking o'er the fretted roof of King's.

Bright and frosty is the morning. Sharp and clear each footfall rings.

Gyps across the court are hurrying with the early breads and butters.

Blithely hums the Master's butler while he's taking down the shutters.

---

[1] New Proctors are as much dreaded in the quadrangles as new ministers in the public offices.

In our rooms we left the kettle gaily singing on the
    coals ;
And within the grate are steaming eggs, and ham, and
    toast, and rolls.
Soon we'll have a jovial breakfast with the members of
    our mess,
Chatting of our darling project, future hopes, and past
    success.
We have come to fetch our brother. What can cause
    his long delay ?
It was not his wont to keep us shivering here the livelong
    day.
He was always sharp and sprightly when the Lion was
    in question ;
Ever ready with an Essay ; ever prompt with a suggestion.

    Surely he must be offended
        At our leaving out his poem :
    Yet no insult was intended,
        As our want of space must show him.
    Or perchance he came home jolly,
        Wishing to knock down the porter,
    And lies cursing at his folly
        With a tongue that tastes like mortar.
    Shew yourself upon the landing :
        Hear your loved companions' groans :
    For our feet are sore with standing
        On the rugged Old Court stones.

           [PHILOLEON *shews himself at the window.*

Phil.—Comrades, when I heard your voices, how my
    heart within me leapt !
Thoughts of happier days came o'er my spirit, and I
    almost wept :—
Those bright days when free and happy with some
    kindred soul I strayed
Talking of The Unconditioned up and down the chesnut
    glade.

                               P

Now a cruel younger brother keeps me under lock and key.

Those I hate are always by me. Those I love I may
not see.

O my own, my cherished Lion, offspring of my cares
and toil,

Would that I and thou were lying underneath the All
Saints' soil !

Drop your voices, dear companions, lest you rouse a
sleeping Bear.

    Chorus A.—Does he then despise our anger ? All men
know who ate Don't Care.

Never fear him ! We'll protect you. Do not heed his
threats and frowns.

Say your prayers, and jump down boldly ! We will
catch you in our gowns.

           [PHILOLEON *places his leg over the window-sill,*
              but is seized from behind by BDELYLEON.

    Bdel.—Not so fast, you old deceiver ! From your evil
courses turn.

Never will I tamely let you join in such a vile concern.

Sooner than behold my brother sunk to such a depth of
scorn

Gladly would I bear to see him walking on a Sunday
morn

'Twixt a pair of pupil-teachers, all the length of Jesus-
lane,

With a school of dirty children slowly shambling in his
train :

Or behold him in the Union, on the Presidential seat,

Shakspeare [1] smiling blandly o'er him, freshmen ranting
at his feet.

Get you gone, you pack of scoundrels ! Don't stand
bawling here all day.

Williams, fetch me out the slop-pail : Jackson, run for
20 K !

---

[1] In the old Union a Shakesperian bust of more than ordinary vapidity
formed a prominent object above the head of the President.

Chorus A.—Slay the despot ! Slay the tyrant ! Him
who cannot brook to see
All his neighbours dwelling round him peaceable, secure,
and free.
Well I know you've long been plotting how to seize the
Castle-hill
With a band of hired assassins, there to work your cruel
will.
Let the man who wrote ' the Syrens ' make a feint upon
the door :
Bring us ladders, ropes, and axes ; we must storm the
second floor.
            [Enter Chorus of First Trinity boating-men.
Chorus B.—Here they are. Upon them boldly !
Double quick across the grass !
Cut them off from Bishop's Hostel, lest along the wall
they pass !
Forward, Darroch ! Forward, Perring ! Charge them,
Lyle, and now remember
'Gainst what odds you fought and conquered on the fifth
of last November :
When you broke with one brave comrade through an
armed and murderous mob.
Fear not an æsthetic humbug, you who've faced a Cam-
bridge snob.
Men of twelve stone, in the centre ! Coxswains, skirmish
on the flank !
You're too eager there, you youngsters : Jones and
Prickard, keep your rank !
Do not stay to spoil the fallen while a soul is left
alive :
We must smoke them out and kill them, now we've
caught them in the hive.
            [They charge the writers in the ' Lion,'
                who fly in all directions.
Victory ! Victory ! now for a shout
As when we bumped the Johnians out !

Vain was the might of Elective Affinities
When brought face to face with our valiant First
    Trinities.
Victory ! Victory ! Huzza ! Tantivy !
      For when a man
      Who can hardly scan
Talks of ' the pictured page of Livy,'
'Tis time for every lad of sense
To arm in honesty's defence
As if the French were steaming over
In rams of iron from Brest to Dover.

        [BDELYLEON *comes out leading* PHILOLEON
        dressed in a First Trinity costume.

Bdel.—Thank you, my brave allies ! And now to
    prove
The confidence I have in your discretion
I here entrust to you my elder brother,
To watch his morals, and to cure his madness.
So treat him kindly ; put him in a tub,
And take him down the river every day ;
And see that no one asks him out to supper,
To make him tipsy. Be not hard upon him,
But let him have his pipe and glass of sherry,
Since he is old and foolish. And, if ever
He comes back sound in body and in mind,
I'll stand you claret at the next club-meeting.

        [*Exit* BDELYLEON.

PARABASIS

We wish to praise our poet, who despising fame and pelf
Flew like a bull-dog at the throat of the jagged toothed
    monster itself,[1]

---

[1] θρασέως συστὰς εὐθὺς ἀπ' ἀρχῆς αὐτῷ καρχαρόδοντι.
        Wasps, line 1031.

Which rages over all the town, from Magdalene-bridge to
    Downing,
With the bray of a dreamy German ass 'neath the hide
    of Robert Browning.
But some of you good fellows think, as the poet grieves
    to hear,
That you are laughed at in ' the Bears,' the play he
    wrote last year :
So he assures you faithfully no insult was intended.
Do not cherish bitter feelings ; for least said is soonest
    mended.

        And next he bids us tax our wit
        To tell some members of the Pitt,
        Whose names he knows not, when they meet
        Him passing into Sidney-street,
        Not to bawl out ' The Bear, The Bear ! '
        First because he does not care :
        Then surely for a man of taste
        It is a sin and shame to waste
        In calling nicknames near the Hoop
        The breath that's given to cool our soup.
        So, being a good-tempered bard,
        Whichever of them leaves his card
        He'll ask him out next week to dine,
        And shake hands o'er a glass of wine.

And now he bids you all good evening, and farewell till
    next October ;
And hopes to-night you'll sup like princes, and that none
    will go home sober.
If policeman K arrests you, let not that your spirits
    damp :
Break his head, and shave his whiskers, and suspend
    him to the lamp.[1]

---

[1] This advice was taken only too literally. The officer in question, on
the night of the First Trinity boat-supper, ventured within the gates of the
college, and was there maltreated in a manner that led, if the author's
recollection serves, to the incarceration of some of the offenders. The
prosecutor commented with much severity upon the concluding lines of
the ' Dionysia.'

Printed in England at THE BALLANTYNE PRESS
SPOTTISWOODE, BALLANTYNE & CO. LTD.
Colchester, London & Eton